The Young Birdwatcher

The Young Birdwatcher

Nicholas Hammond

Hamlyn
London · New York · Sydney · Toronto

Acknowledgments

Illustrations by Ian Willis and Robert Morton
Identification plates by Ian Willis

Colour photographs
Ardea Photographics title page; Frank V. Blackburn 30 top,
31 top, 31 centre, 31 bottom left, 31 bottom right, 34, 35 top,
35 bottom, 54, 55 top, 55 bottom, 58 bottom left, 58 bottom
right, 59 top, 59 centre left, 59 centre right, 59 bottom left,
59 bottom right, 70, 71 top, 71 bottom left, 71 bottom right,
78 bottom left, 78 bottom right, 79 top, 79 bottom left, 101;
Bruce Coleman Limited 26; David Hosking 27 bottom; Eric
Hosking 86; Natural History Photographic Agency – Stephen
Dalton 27 top; Natural History Photographic Agency – D. N.
Dalton 30 bottom; Royal Society for the Protection of Birds
– Michael W. Richards 79 bottom right, 87; I. Wyllie 66
bottom left, 66 bottom right, 67 top right, 67 centre, 67 bottom.

Black-and-white photographs
Frank V. Blackburn 76, 77; Udo Hirsch 56 top left, 56 top
right, 56 bottom left, 56 bottom right, 57; Frank W. Lane
half title page, 53; Royal Society for the Protection of Birds –
Richard Porter 88; Royal Society for the Protection of Birds
– Michael W. Richards 64, 69; Royal Society for the Protection of Birds – Arne Schmitz 81.

Published 1978 by
The Hamlyn Publishing Group Limited
London · New York · Sydney · Toronto
Astronaut House, Feltham, Middlesex, England
© Copyright The Hamlyn Publishing Group Limited 1978

ISBN 0 600 31433 2

Printed in Italy

Contents

Introduction

More popular in Europe than any other form of wildlife study, ornithology, the study of birds, can be followed all year round. Birds may be found almost anywhere, even in the centre of cities. They can be seen throughout the year, but some move away in winter whilst others appear.

About six hundred species have been recorded in Europe and about four hundred breed regularly. These vary in size from the tiny goldcrest at 9 cm long to the huge whooper swan with a length of 152 cm and a wingspan of 250 cm.

The variations in size are matched by the difference in shape, feeding habits, nests and habitats. Habitats are the places where birds live.

This book is divided into three main sections: the biology and behaviour of birds, how to set about studying them, and how to identify them. In addition, there are a list of the European species most likely to be seen and a glossary of terms which are used in ornithology and appear throughout this book.

White stork

Spoonbill

Mute swan

Pintail

Avocet

The word 'species' is used frequently in this book. A species is a group of birds that interbreed and produce young that will grow up to breed successfully. While different species may breed in captivity, their offspring are often sterile or unable to breed.

Different species such as the song thrush and the mistle thrush may look very alike and may be found in the same places, but they do not interbreed. Look carefully and you will see that the song thrush is smaller. It also eats slightly different food and chooses different nest sites.

Both are members of the same genus, (plural-genera), which is a group of species that display similar characteristics in the development

of their bodies. There may be several genera in the same family which is the next group. Families are part of an even larger group known as an order. The song and mistle thrushes are members of the genus of true thrushes. True thrushes and several other genera, including warblers, chats, flycatchers and wrens are members of the family *Muscicapidae*. This family is part of the very large order *Passeriformes*, or perching birds, frequently referred to as passerines.

Species are separated from each other as a result of a process called evolution. This process is still going on but it takes such a long time to

happen that we are not aware of it. Each species has adapted to make the best possible use of the place where it lives, its habitat. This process is called adaptive radiation. Often, species that appear very similar may be seen in the same habitat, but they do not feed on the same food. For example, you will often see the greylag goose and pink-footed goose feeding together

Birds come in many shapes and sizes, and all are perfectly adapted for their chosen habitats.

in the same places, but if you look closely you will see that they are eating different food. Both eat root crops but the smaller bill of the pinkfoot cannot handle large vegetables such as potatoes, which the greylag is able to eat.

How Birds Began

Like reptiles, amphibians, fish and mammals, birds have skeletons inside their bodies. But what makes birds different from other vertebrates?

They fly, of course, but so do bats, which are mammals. And remember that some birds do not fly, such as ostriches and penguins. Birds lay eggs, but so do fish, reptiles and two very primitive species of Australian mammal.

There is one feature that birds do not share with any other animal – feathers. No other class of animal has feathers, and how they actually developed in birds is not clear, like so much else in ornithology. One of the problems with researching into feathers is that no one is absolutely sure just how birds evolved.

Did they evolve directly from reptiles? Or did they, as some scientists now think, come from the extinct dinosaurs? If this is the case, the questions still to be answered are how and when this happened.

Archaeopteryx

The earliest known animal with feathers is the Archaeopteryx, which lived about 150 million years ago. Far from being a huge monster like so many prehistoric creatures, it was about the size of a magpie. We know about Archaeopteryx because of fossil finds in Bavaria

during the last century. Three fossils were found where limestone was being quarried for lithographic printing. One of these fossils is now in the British Museum (Natural History) in London, and the other two are in German museums.

Archaeopteryx – about the size of a magpie – represented a link between the reptiles and the birds.

Some features of Archaeopteryx are similar to modern birds. In fact, the feathers do not seem in any way different in construction from those of modern birds. Also, the four toes, with three pointing forward and one pointing back, are very similar to the feet of modern perching birds. However, some of the features of Archaeopteryx, such as the structure of some of its bones and its brain, are similar to those of reptiles. It appears that this 'bird-reptile' is a link between the two classes, as major groups of animals are called.

Unfortunately, fossil remains of land birds are rarely found. Land birds that died were usually eaten by other animals, while sea-creatures or their skeletons sank to the bottom and were preserved in the salt ooze on the sea-bed.

Odd bone fossils of bird-like creatures have been found from the Cretaceous Age (75–125 million years ago). It was then that the dinosaurs disappeared, and from that period we also have our first record of a bird that could fly by itself. This was something that Archaeopteryx could not do; although it had wings, it lacked the deep keel-shaped breast bone needed to anchor powerful wing muscles. Without these wing muscles, Archaeopteryx could not lift itself off the ground, even with a run. However, it might have been able to use its wings to glide from the treetops, having clambered up with the help of its feet and the claws on its wings.

Ichthyornis, the first flying bird.

Ichthyornis

The first flying bird is called Ichthyornis. A small sea-bird,

rather like the modern terns, it lived about 80 million years ago.

Hesperornis

At about the same time, there was a flightless swimming bird called Hesperornis, whose legs and feet were so highly adapted to swimming that it was probably unable to walk on land. It must have been quite a bird, because it was 2 metres long from the tip of its bill to its tail.

Hesperornis was a large flightless bird which lived about 80 million years ago.

A few other species of prehistoric bird have been identified from the same period by experts who have worked from the fossils of a few bones and built up a picture of the birds as they were. It is a pity that no one was around to draw pictures when these birds were alive. By the time man first appeared, between 1 and 2 million years ago, most modern families of birds had existed for several million years and the Archaeopteryx, Ichthyornis and Hesperornis were extinct.

Birds in Europe today

The main groups into which birds are divided are called 'orders'. In the world there are 29 orders of which 18 are represented in Europe.

Great crested grebe

Great northern diver

Fulmar

Gannet

Heron

Mallard

Capercaillie

Peregrine

Examples of species from the orders of European birds.

Moorhen

Oystercatcher

Cuckoo

Turtle dove

Snowy owl

Nightjar

Bee-eater

Swift

Black woodpecker

Blackbird

Structure & Function of Feathers

Although we may not be sure exactly how birds' feathers evolved from the scales of reptiles, we do know something about the structure and function of the feathers of modern birds. They are an aid to flight, keep the bird's body heat in and the cold out, protect the bird through camouflage and make the bird attractive to others of the same species through display.

The structure of feathers

If you compare a plucked chicken with a live one you will see just how much difference feathers make to

the shape of a bird. On your plucked chicken you will notice small bumps all over the skin; these are the follicles from which the feathers grow, and they stand up because they have been drawn upwards as the feathers have been plucked. They are really cavities in the skin in which the feathers grow.

The main part of the feather is a shaft from which the vanes or barbs of the feather grow. One end of the shaft is bare, and pointed – this is the part that is within the skin. A cross-section of this part shows that it is circular whilst the other end, which is longer and supports the

A feather grows from a depression in the skin, known as a follicle.

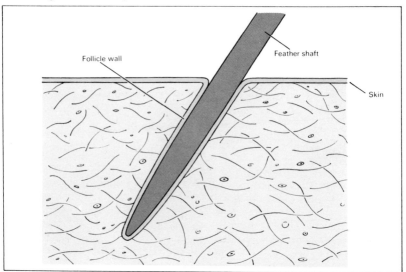

Follicle wall

Feather shaft

Skin

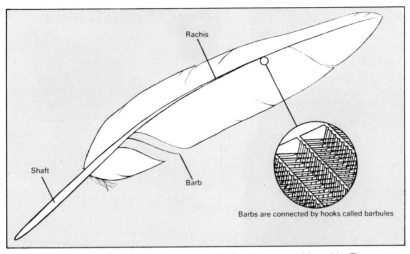

The parts of a feather. It consists of a central shaft with a vane either side. The vanes consist of a series of barbs.

vanes, is quadrangular. The vanes occur on opposite sides of the shaft, but they are not always of equal length. They are often shorter on one side where feathers overlap, in the way that the sections of feather-board fencing overlap.

Vanes are held in place by barbs, which in turn are held in place by small hooks called barbules. This provides a net-like pattern that can be seen in the illustration of a primary feather, one of the main flight feathers.

Numbers of feathers

Not all species have the same number of feathers, and the number of contour feathers may alter at different times of the year. The number in house sparrows varies by almost 10% in a year, from 3,200 in summer to 3,500 in winter. In tropical countries, where there is little seasonal change in the climate, there is correspondingly little change in the number of feathers in an individual bird throughout the whole year.

Record-holders for the number of feathers are the swans, which have over 25,000. At the other end of the scale are the small perching birds that we see in gardens, with between 1,500 and 3,500 feathers. Although this may not seem a great number compared with the feathers of a swan, remember that these birds are very much smaller and have more feathers per square centimetre of body area, because they need more insulation.

Feather care

Feathers must be kept in first-class condition. In addition to the moult of old and worn feathers, the bird must constantly look after its plumage. It does this in various ways. The method of feather care most usually seen is *preening*. The bird takes a feather at the base and draws it through its bill. This cleans off dirt and lice, fits the barbs and barbules in place and smooths the plumage.

Oystercatcher preening.

Head-scratching

Head-scratching with the foot is the way in which the bird reaches an area its bill cannot reach. When you watch birds you will notice that different groups use their feet in different ways – some just raise their feet directly to their heads, while others tuck their feet behind their wings to reach their heads.

Herring gull direct scratching.

Blackbird indirect scratching.

Bathing

Bathing is another way in which birds care for their feathers. Water-birds and waders push their heads and necks into the water; land-birds use shallow water in puddles and at pond edges and dunk their throats and necks; and the swallows and martins, which spend much of their time in the air, bathe by flying very low over the water and dipping their breasts and throats in it.

Starling bathing.

Oil glands

Most birds have oil glands on the rump. Some use this gland for preening by extracting the oil from the gland with the bill and smearing it on their plumage.

This jay is allowing ants to crawl over its body. This is called indirect anting.

Oiling, as shown here by a song thrush, helps to waterproof the plumage.

Dusting

Where there is fine, dry soil, some birds will make a hollow in the earth and, pressing their bodies into the hollow, will spread the dust with their wings. No one really knows the function of dusting, but it is thought that it might be to dislodge parasites.

the ants to crawl over its body. Ants produce formic acid and it is thought that this acid will either destroy feather-lice or proof the plumage against lice in the way that moth-balls are used to keep moths away from clothes. In place of ants, birds may use such unusual items as burning cigarette ends, mustard or citrus fruits.

Direct anting is when a bird, here a starling, picks up ants and puts them in its plumage.

A house sparrow dusting.

Anting

Even more curious behaviour is anting. The bird will find an ant colony and either pick up the ants in its bill and place them in its plumage, or flop down on the ant-hill and allow

Sunning

On very hot days you may notice birds lying in the sun with their feathers fluffed out and their wings outspread. This is called sunning and may be a form of feather care or a method of reducing the heat trapped beneath a bird's feathers.

Types of feather

There are six types of feathers, each of which performs a particular job:

Contours

These are the stiff feathers that give the bird its shape. Wing feathers are typical contours. Others are modified for special purposes; for example, the stiffened tail feathers of woodpeckers help the bird to keep its balance against a tree trunk. Others may be ornamental, such as the plumes of egrets or the tail feathers of peacocks.

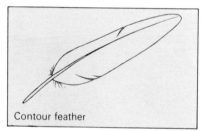

Contour feather

Semi-plumes

These are the small, downy feathers that help to trap warm air close to the bird's body, in the way that a string vest traps pockets of air against human skin.

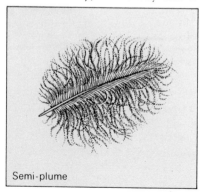

Semi-plume

Down

This is even finer than semi-plumes and also helps to trap air. It is very important in water-birds because the trapped air helps to keep the bird afloat.

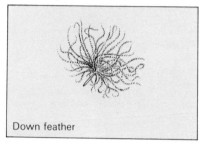

Down feather

Filoplumes

These are small, fine feathers found at the base of contour feathers. We do not know what function they perform but they may be connected with receiving vibrations. These vibrations cause the muscles controlling contour feathers to act.

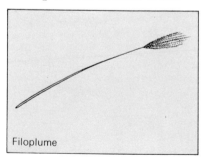

Filoplume

Bristles

These are specialised feathers found around the bills of some species, such as nightjars. They are used as feelers in a similar way to whiskers in mammals.

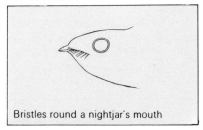

Bristles round a nightjar's mouth

Powder-down

This down produces a very fine powder which helps to waterproof plumage. It is found in several species, such as herons, parrots and pigeons.

Moulting

Anyone who has a dog knows that at certain times of year it moults to get rid of old hair and make way for the new. The same happens to birds' feathers. All the feathers could not fall out at the same time or the bird could not survive. It is a gradual process that takes some weeks. The first moult occurs when the natal down, which is already on the chick when it hatches or which grows soon after hatching, is pushed out by the new feathers of the juvenile plumage. The moults that follow take place in a slightly different way, because the old feathers fall out and are replaced by the new feathers and not pushed out by them. The next moult is in the autumn of the first year when the bird takes on its first winter plum-age. This is replaced in spring by the breeding plumage and in its second winter it takes on its winter plumage. So the cycle of twice yearly moults continues.

Not all species follow this pattern and there is variation between groups. The ptarmigan, for instance, needs three moults a year, because it lives in mountains where the amount of snow varies with the seasons. In winter, the ptarmigan is almost entirely white, to merge with the colour of the snow. In the spring, as the snow melts and the rocks and plants begin to show through, it becomes white and grey-brown. In summer, when the snow has disappeared, the bird becomes brown.

Ducks go through a summer moult known as an eclipse. This usually begins in late June or July with the body feathers, and is followed by the moulting of wing and tail feathers. During this time they cannot fly, so they are more vulnerable and become very shy, keeping to cover. Males lose their bright plumage and look very like females. However, if you look carefully you can sort out the eclipse males from the females because they have traces of their normal pattern in their plumage. Looking for male ducks in eclipse on town park lakes is very good practice and will help you to make lightning identifications of ducks at other times of the year, because you will learn to recognise their shapes.

Taking to the Air

Man has tried to imitate birds for hundreds of years. Some years ago a large sum of money was offered to the first person who could fly under his own power. Only one man has ever managed it. There are three forces that man has always had to contend with, and they are forces that he is just not built to overcome. They are drag (the resistance of the air), the force of gravity and the turbulence caused by movement.

Structure for flying

Birds have evolved to overcome these forces in several ways. Their bones are almost hollow, and honeycombed with chambers of air to give lightness. Also many are fused together instead of being socketed and held in place by muscles as our bones are.

The deep, keel-shaped breastbone, called the sternum, has developed to anchor the very powerful muscles that move the wings. At the end of the spine there is a fused bone called the pygostyle. This is an anchor for the tail, which is very important in flight. These adaptions give a bird the power to overcome the downward pull of gravity.

By flapping its wings in a partially circular motion, the bird can obtain lift against the force of gravity. To overcome drag, the leading edge of the wing is thicker than the trailing edge, giving a tapering effect and allowing the air to pass off the trailing edge of the wing.

Birds have evolved into very efficient flying machines. To enable them to fly, their bones are constructed in a different way from other vertebrates, and the arrangement of the bones has produced a skeleton specially adapted for flight.

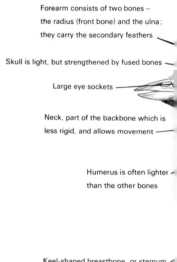

Forearm consists of two bones – the radius (front bone) and the ulna; they carry the secondary feathers

Skull is light, but strengthened by fused bones

Large eye sockets

Neck, part of the backbone which is less rigid, and allows movement

Humerus is often lighter than the other bones

Keel-shaped breastbone, or sternum, is an anchorage for the very powerful muscles that operate the wings

The movement of the wing will create turbulence in the air, but this is overcome by the arrangement and structure of the feathers. These enable the wing to make an airtight, unbroken surface on the downward stroke, but to open and allow the air to pass through it on the upward stroke.

Flying does not only involve wings. Other parts of the body are important too. Legs, for instance, are vital to take-off, and must be strong for the bird's spring into the air from a perch or the ground. Exceptions are members of the swift family which spend most of their lives in the air and nest in the cre-

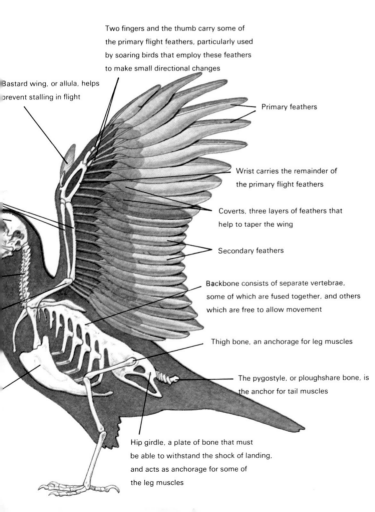

Two fingers and the thumb carry some of the primary flight feathers, particularly used by soaring birds that employ these feathers to make small directional changes

Bastard wing, or allula, helps prevent stalling in flight

Primary feathers

Wrist carries the remainder of the primary flight feathers

Coverts, three layers of feathers that help to taper the wing

Secondary feathers

Backbone consists of separate vertebrae, some of which are fused together, and others which are free to allow movement

Thigh bone, an anchorage for leg muscles

The pygostyle, or ploughshare bone, is the anchor for tail muscles

Hip girdle, a plate of bone that must be able to withstand the shock of landing, and acts as anchorage for some of the leg muscles

Water birds, such as the mute swan, paddle along the surface and flap their wings to take off.

The powerful downstroke provides lift, with feathers closed flat to push against the air.

vices of roof-eaves. They have very short legs and have difficulty if they are grounded, because they do not have sufficient spring to get airborne again. Some heavy birds must take a run to become airborne; when swans take off they look as though they are running across the surface of the water.

Performance in the air

Once in the air, a bird's performance depends on the species. Some hardly fly at all because the way in which they live does not necessitate it. Others are experts in the air. The long-distance specialists have developed the power to fly for long periods and make the most of air currents. Some must be able to twist and turn at speed to catch birds on which they feed or to avoid being caught by other birds.

Looking at the shape of a bird's wings and tail can give us a number of clues about how it lives.

If we compare the flight shape of the sparrowhawk and kestrel, we can see how they differ according to their hunting methods. Both are

The inner part of the wing keeps the bird in the air by the air rushing over it and maintaining lift, and the 'fingers', or primaries, twist and push the bird forward. The wings are swept forward at the end of the downstroke.

On the upstroke the feathers fan out to reduce air-resistance. The wing-tips go through a figure of eight in each complete cycle.

Land birds, such as the blackbird, take off by jumping into the air, and flapping their wings to create lift.

rather small for birds of prey, about 34 cm long, and both are found throughout Europe. The sparrowhawk has broad, 'fingered' wings and a long, broad tail. This is because it hunts small birds along hedgerows and woodland edges and needs to be able to manoeuvre quickly to catch them. The kestrel, on the other hand, has long, pointed wings and a long tail. Rather than dashing after its prey, like the sparrowhawk, the kestrel hovers above open country waiting to spot a movement in the grass, which may be one of the small rodents

Like other parts of the bird, its wings have evolved to be the most suitable shape for its habitat.

Broad wings of the griffon vulture allow it to soar high above the ground, looking for food

Pointed, rapidly beating wings like the teal's help it rise and move off very quickly

which it hunts. Once it has spotted the prey, the kestrel swoops down using its pointed wings, which are streamlined for speed.

There are interesting differences between two even more familiar species – the swallow and house martin. Both are summer migrants, nesting in or on man's buildings, and both feed on flying insects caught in their mouths in flight. Both have narrow, pointed wings for fast flight, but the tail and wings of the swallow are longer because the swallow feeds nearer the ground than the house martin. As it skims low over the ground it needs to change direction very rapidly to avoid such obstacles as bushes and cows. The swallow's ability to manoeuvre in the air enables it to nest in places that are even more difficult to reach than the eaves under which the house martin nests.

Pheasant's broad, round wings and long tail allow it maximum manoeuvrability in woodland

Partridge lives in open country and needs to fly fast, but does not need the manoeuvrability of the pheasant

Fulmar has long, straight wings which act like the wings of a glider, keeping the bird airborne with as little effort as possible

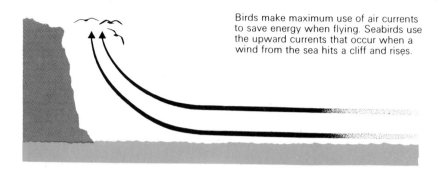

Birds make maximum use of air currents to save energy when flying. Seabirds use the upward currents that occur when a wind from the sea hits a cliff and rises.

Air currents and winds

Birds that travel long distances in search of their food take advantage of the air currents caused by differences in the temperature of the air. Warm air is pushed up by cold air and because the earth's surface heats up unevenly, columns of rising warm air called thermals are produced. Long-distance migrants, such as some eagles and storks, make use of thermals when they are migrating. Their broad wings provide a large surface that can be lifted by the warm air. The

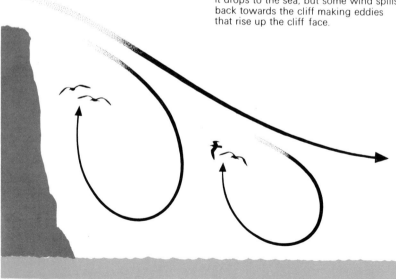

When an offshore wind comes to a cliff it drops to the sea, but some wind spills back towards the cliff making eddies that rise up the cliff face.

'fingered' wings and broad tails help the bird's manoeuvrability so that it can keep in the thermal.

Air currents caused by the wind can be very useful to birds. A sea wind will rise when it hits a cliff, and birds will make use of this updraught to gain height. An offshore wind does not drop down immediately it reaches the cliff top. Instead it drops gently down to the sea and air currents spill back towards, and up, the cliff face. Birds take advantage of these small air currents to rise upwards.

Out at sea, winds slow down near the surface. They reach their maximum speed at 12 to 24 metres above the sea. Seabirds, such as gannets, manx shearwaters and fulmars, with their long, thin wings, use these differences in wind speeds. The bird uses the fastest part of the wind to build up great speed as it flies down at a shallow angle towards the surface. Then, using its momentum, it wheels upward against the wind. Wings act as aerofoils, the air-resisting surfaces of an aeroplane, and long, thin ones are ideal for this sort of flight, as the design for gliders shows.

Tails are very important in flight because they are the main means of steering. By moving the tail the bird can change direction. Species with short tails are those that do not need to change direction rapidly.

Winds move slower near the surface of the sea. Therefore gliding seabirds, such as albatrosses and petrels, can rise and fall, by wheeling steeply against the wind.

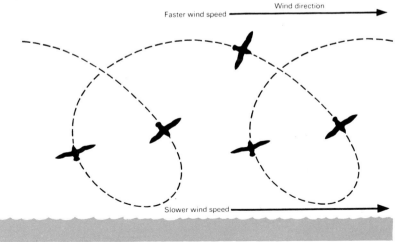

Wind direction

Faster wind speed

Slower wind speed

Landing

One of the most difficult tasks of an aeroplane pilot is landing. Landing can be difficult for young birds too, and they learn how to do it successfully only by trial and error. By the time they are adults they are so skilful that we tend to take their expertise for granted. But landing is a complex business. Just as an aeroplane must lose speed when it lands, so must a bird. It brakes by spreading its wings and tail. Large, heavy birds generally reduce speed by landing into the wind, and waterbirds spread their webbed feet to brake against the water. Woodland birds, which often fly to perch in trees, have a dipping flight with fre-

Left The webbed feet of these mallard are used as brakes against the water, and the wings are held out to assist slowing down.

Above Feet and tails are important in helping a bird to land. The tail of this tawny owl is fanned out and the wings are held back. The legs help absorb the shock of landing.

Right This heron landing in a tree flaps its wings until it has slowed sufficiently to drop onto the branches.

quent bouts of gentle gliding. As they approach a tree they glide downwards and then upwards towards the perch, losing speed.

Bird Senses

To study birds we must try to understand how their minds work. It is very easy to imagine that they think in the same way as we do, especially when their behaviour seems to be almost human. Unlike us, they have no interest in anything but themselves. Their minds are totally committed to survival, through food, safety from danger, and reproduction. They have no emotions of faith, hope or charity, bravery or cowardice, kindness or cruelty.

Like us, birds have the senses of sight, hearing, smell, taste and touch. But each of these senses is developed to a different extent.

Eyesight

The eyesight of birds is highly developed. The eyes themselves are very large; some owls have eyes as big as a man's and the ostrich's eyes are even bigger, with a diameter of 5 cm. A bird's eye is often as big and as heavy as its brain.

Such big, eyes occupy a large space in the skull and they almost touch. This means that there is little room left for the muscles that move the eyeball and so, birds have very limited eyeball movement. Instead they have considerable movement in the neck to allow them all-round vision. Some species of owls can move their necks through 270° very quickly. If you walk around a perched owl it will follow you by turning its head in an almost circular movement, and if you continue walking, it will whip its head back rapidly so that it can still see you.

Inside the eye there are pole-shaped bodies called rods, which are sensitive to light and particularly numerous in nocturnal birds, such as owls and nightjars. Birds also have cones, which are colour sensitive bodies in the retina of the eye; only a few mammals, including humans, have cones.

Eyes are important and need protection. As well as two eyelids, birds have a special device called a nictitating membrane, which comes across the eyeball to clean it. Owls, like humans, close their eyes by bringing down their upper eyelids, but most birds can only close the lower lids.

Compare these skulls of a squirrel and a pigeon. Notice how much larger the pigeon's eye sockets are.

Squirrel

Pigeon

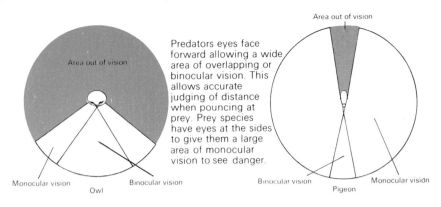

Predators eyes face forward allowing a wide area of overlapping or binocular vision. This allows accurate judging of distance when pouncing at prey. Prey species have eyes at the sides to give them a large area of monocular vision to see danger.

Owl

Area out of vision

Monocular vision

Binocular vision

Pigeon

Area out of vision

Binocular vision

Monocular vision

Anyone who has tried swimming underwater knows that it can be very difficult to see, and yet many species swim underwater to find food. Kingfishers which catch fish beneath the surface can see as well underwater as above it. Many water-birds have little windows in their nictitating membranes to act like underwater contact lenses.

The position of the eyes in the skull depends on the feeding habits of the bird. Birds of prey tend to have their eyes in the front of the skull so that they can see their prey when they are chasing them. The birds that are chased need to be able to see what is happening behind them and to either side, so their eyes are positioned at the sides of their skull. Woodcock are extreme examples of this, and they can see just as well behind as in front.

Having eyes at the sides of the head means that the bird can see a separate image with each eye. This is called monocular vision. When both eyes look forward they can both focus together, as ours do. This is called binocular vision. Owls have binocular vision to an angle of 60° to 70°, while finches have an angle of vision of under 25°.

Hearing

Acute hearing is as important to birds as good eyesight. A bird's ears are situated on the side of the head in a similar position to the ears of mammals, but a bird does not have fleshy ears as a human does.

The safety of a bird may depend on being able to detect the approach of a predator or the alarm calls of other birds. It is also important for it to hear the songs of other birds. Birds can pick up a greater frequency of sound than we can. The rapid song of the tiny wren is so fast that the human ear cannot pick out all the notes, but other wrens' ears can.

Balance

A sense of balance is dependent on the ear, too. People with a damaged inner ear may find it difficult to keep their balance. Without the ability to balance, a bird would find movement on the ground or in the air very difficult, and the intricate manoeuvre of landing would be an impossibility.

Smell

Mammals rely very greatly on a sense of smell and for this reason they have highly developed olfactory bulbs, which are the organs that control the sense of smell. In most birds these organs are small and experiments have suggested that a sense of smell plays very little part in the bird's food-finding. One exception is the kiwi, a flightless nocturnal bird from New Zealand, whose sense of smell is very highly developed and helps it to find its food of grubs and insects.

Taste

Taste is very important to those of us who enjoy our food. We taste through nerve-ends known as tastebuds, which, as in most mammals, are situated mainly on our tongue. Humans have almost 10,000 tastebuds and rabbits 17,000, whereas most birds have from 40 to 60. In birds they are situated mainly in the throat rather than the tongue.

Birds avoid eating food that tastes unpleasant. Some amphibians, such as newts and salamanders, taste unpleasant, and display aposematic or warning colours of yellow and black. These are also the colours of wasps, which few birds try to eat more than once. Other harmless insects have adapted to imitate warning colours so that birds will avoid them too.

Instincts

Much of birds' behaviour is instinctive. Behaviour experts believe that a bird has six basic instincts: food, fighting, reproduction, social relations, sleep and the care of body surfaces.

1

1 The barn owl instinctively searches for voles.
2 This goldfinch is defending its territory against another.

2

3

3 Copulation, as shown by these nuthatches, is also instinctive.

4 Social relations are shown by these moorhens preening each other.

5 A sleeping little owl.

6 Care of the body surfaces is very important, and this song thrush is dust bathing to remove parasites from its feathers.

4

5

6

These instincts may arise in a number of ways. They are inherited from the bird's parents, usually stimulated by complicated, internal chemical changes within the bird or by outside events. They are complex and often rigid in their pattern. One of the best examples of instinct and how it works is shown in the mating behaviour of birds. Mating behaviour is triggered by climatic conditions, which affect the birds so that males and females react to each other instinctively. Outside the breeding season they may not react to each other at all.

Learning ability

In addition, birds do have learning ability. It is easy to confuse learning ability with intelligence, which is the ability to reason. The degree of learning ability depends on the development of the species. Thus, the more primitive birds, such as divers and grebes, do not have a very high ability to learn compared with the highly developed sparrows and members of the crow family.

Learning ability shows itself in various ways. The first is habituation, through which the bird learns not to react to certain situations. For instance, a young bird assumes that anything else that moves is dangerous, but will soon learn that certain animals, such as butterflies, are harmless. Trial and error is another form of learning and birds rely on it for certain activities, such

as nest-building. Sometimes birds solve problems without resorting to trial and error. These are cases of insight learning, perhaps the ability most closely resembling intelligence. An example of insight learning is the way in which some birds, with apparently very little thought, will pull up a string of peanuts from above in order to reach the nuts.

Recognising numbers of objects

The ability to count is so easily acquired by people that we often assume that animals share it. In fact, birds and animals do not count but some can recognise numbers of objects. Many species, though, cannot really distinguish between two or more objects. Corvids, members of the crow family, can distinguish between three and four objects, four and five, five and six, and six and seven. This is a similar ability to that of humans.

Imprinting

Finally, there is imprinting. This happens with birds hatched in incubators and kept away from adults of the same species. Geese hatched in this way will become imprinted on humans; they will ignore other geese and direct mating displays at human beings. It is thought that song is learned through imprinting of the parents' song on the young.

How Birds Feed

Food and cover are important to birds and these are the basic requirements for the habitat of any species. Some birds are found in one particular habitat. For instance, the bittern only breeds in reed-marshes. Others are not so choosy and the carrion crow, which eats almost anything, is an example of a species found in almost all European habitats.

The main types of habitat in Europe are sea, seashore and estuaries, sea-cliffs, slow-running rivers, salt marshes, freshwater marshes, coniferous woodland, broadleaved woodland, heathland, woodland edges, farmland, gardens and parkland, scrub, fast-running rivers, moorland, mountains and tundra. Each of these could be sub-divided further but the list is sufficient for general reference.

Adaptation

To make the most of its environment a bird must adapt. It does this in a number of ways. The webbed feet of ducks and other water-birds are some of the most obvious adaptations to the birds' habitat.

Bird's feet differ according to the way each lives.

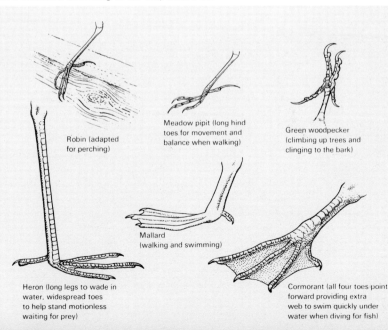

Robin (adapted for perching)

Meadow pipit (long hind toes for movement and balance when walking)

Green woodpecker (climbing up trees and clinging to the bark)

Mallard (walking and swimming)

Heron (long legs to wade in water, widespread toes to help stand motionless waiting for prey)

Cormorant (all four toes point forward providing extra web to swim quickly under water when diving for fish)

These have developed to enable the birds to swim better. But there are adaptations in almost all species. Perching birds have feet that are adapted to perching, with three toes pointing forward and one pointing backward. Some passerine species do not spend very much time in trees, finding food and places to nest on the ground. Of these, some prefer grassy places and hop, while others prefer flatter areas and move on the ground by running. Woodpeckers depend on trees for their nest-sites and spend much of their time clinging to treebark looking for insect food. Their feet, therefore, have developed so that two toes point forward and two backward. These are known as zygodactylic feet.

Colouring

Colour of plumage is also related to the habitat chosen by birds. Ground-nesting species must merge into their surroundings if they are not to be spotted by foxes and other predators. The nightjar, which is a nocturnal bird, nests on the ground in its habitat of heathland and woodland edges. During the day they would be in danger if they did not merge into their background. As it is, they are very difficult to find because their brown and grey plumage is hard to distinguish from the dead leaves and branches on the ground. This is a marvellous example of camouflage.

Another form of protective coloration is disruptive colouring. An example of this occurs in the male

The nightjar's camouflage colouring makes it very difficult to see against the background of its habitat, since it resembles a piece of dead wood.

wheatear. With its grey head and back, black eye-stripe, black wings, white rump and black tail, it stands out well against a plain background, but against the rough rocks on a mountain-side, which present areas of light and shade, it disappears. This is because its bold contrasting pattern disrupts its outline when seen against a background in which there is plenty of light and shade. Another bird whose colour is disruptive is the magpie, which is easy to spot against the background of a field of grass but is often difficult to see when it is high in the bough of a tree in winter. If you look through the illustrations at the back of this book, you may be able to guess the habitat of many birds by their colouring.

The bold, contrasting markings of the wheatear (*above*) and magpie (*below*) break up their outlines and make them hard to see. This is called disruptive coloration.

The best clue to the food of a particular bird is its bill. Certain types of bill can be easily distinguished.

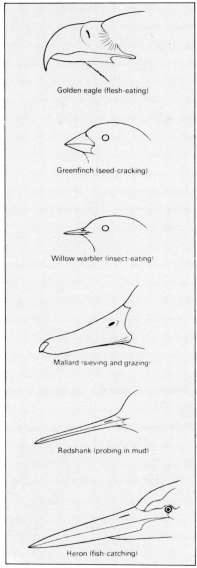

Golden eagle (flesh-eating)

Greenfinch (seed-cracking)

Willow warbler (insect-eating)

Mallard (sieving and grazing)

Redshank (probing in mud)

Heron (fish-catching)

Feeding

The way in which birds feed determines their shape. The shape of the bill is an obvious guide to the sort of food and how a bird eats. There are several main types of bill: flesh-eating, probing, insect-eating, seed-eating, fruit-eating and fish-catching.

Within these types there are differences. Among the flesh-eaters, the size and shape of the bill varies between species according to the food taken, but all are hooked. Although many birds of prey catch and kill their prey, some such as the vultures feed on carrion, animals that are already dead when they find them. For this they need rather long bills and necks to probe among the carcases on which they feed. To make life easier, most species of vulture have no feathers on the head, such as the black vulture, or very short down on the head, such as the griffon vulture; this stops the head becoming matted with blood and pieces of flesh as it probes about inside the carcase.

Most of the predators catch their prey with their feet, using their sharp claws or talons. The osprey, which catches fish in its talons, has tiny spikes on the underside of each foot which help the bird to grip the fish and not drop it as it carries it away. If it plunged into water to catch fish, the osprey would have problems with wet feathers, and for this reason the feathers on its lower breast are waterproofed.

Although all are flesh-eaters, birds of prey have adapted to deal with particular types of food.

Honey buzzard feeds mainly on wasp and bee grubs with its sharp, delicate bill. Hard feathers round its face protect it from stings

Osprey has a slit-shaped nostril which can be closed when the bird dives in the water after fish

Head of black vulture is only partially feathered, as feathers would become matted with blood when tearing at carrion

Egyptian vulture also eats carrion, but has smaller bill to reach the pieces of flesh that larger vultures cannot reach

Wading birds feed on small invertebrates that live several centimetres below the mud on sea-shores and estuaries. To reach them, waders, such as the redshank and curlew, need long probing bills. If you look at the illustrations of waders on pages 146 to 151, you will notice that the bills all differ in length and shape. This is because they feed at different depths in the mud on different invertebrates. You will also see that they all have long-ish legs, which, with their longish necks, enable them to feed when the mud is covered by shallow water.

Many wading birds spend their winters feeding in estuaries and on coastal mudflats. To avoid competition for food, each species has adapted to feed in a different way, as can be seen by the different bills.

Curlew's long bill probes mud even deeper than godwit's

Bar-tailed godwit uses long bill for probing the mud for burrowing shellfish and worms

Ringed plover's short bill is used for snatching small animals in the shallows or on the mud

Oystercatcher has heavy bill for prising shells from rocks and crushing them

Redshank has all-purpose bill for probing mud, dislodging pebbles and snatching moving prey

Turnstone has short bill for dislodging pebbles to find small animals

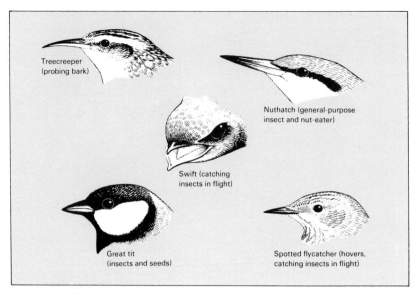

Insect-eating birds usually have pointed, rather thin bills, but just as insects come in many different sizes, shapes and habitats, so insect-eaters have a wide variety of bills to cope with them.

Birds that eat insects have thin, pointed bills. They can carry several insects in their bills at the same time, which is very useful when they have a nestful of hungry young to feed. Variations in the bills of insect-eaters give some clue as to how they find their food. A woodland species, the treecreeper, has a down-curved, longish bill with which it probes for insects among crevices in tree bark. The nuthatch, another small woodland species often seen on tree bark, has a longer, pointed bill which is used to probe for insects and seeds; it also eats nuts, which it wedges in crevices in the bark and opens by striking them

hard with its bill. Birds that eat flying insects have wide, gaping bills which make it easy for them to catch their prey while they are in flight.

Seed-eaters have bills that are pointed at the tip and broad at the base. The bills of finches are typically adapted to cracking seeds. The upper mandible has a groove and the lower mandible fits into it. A seed is fitted into the groove and held with the tongue and the lower mandible is brought up to crush the seed husk.

Each species of finch shows different bill shapes. These vary according to what food the species takes. The goldfinch's bill is longer and rather more pointed than those of other European finches. It is perfectly adapted to extract and crush seeds from the heads of thistles and teazels. To balance on thistle heads waving in the autumn wind, the goldfinch must be slender and agile. Even more agile is the redpoll – it feeds on the seeds of alders, which it reaches by hanging upside down on the old fruit growing at the ends of branches.

The hawfinch has a massive bill, heavy and powerful enough to crush stones of cherries, olives and sloes. Inside the bill are a pair of knobs on each mandible. These, with the powerful muscles that operate the jaws, help to distribute the shock of cracking stones through the skull. An enormous force is needed to crack a cherry stone. In fact, experiments have shown that to split a cherry stone one must apply a load of over 44 kilos. When you realise that the hawfinch itself weighs only 55 grammes, such power is quite remarkable.

All finches have basic seed-eating bills, but each species shows adaptations to deal with its particular food.

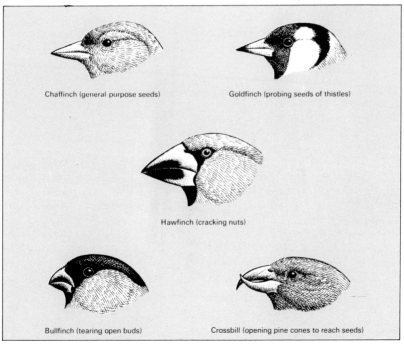

Chaffinch (general purpose seeds)

Goldfinch (probing seeds of thistles)

Hawfinch (cracking nuts)

Bullfinch (tearing open buds)

Crossbill (opening pine cones to reach seeds)

Deciduous woodland once covered much of lowland Europe. Very little of the original woodland remains, but birds still occupy particular niches here.

Treecreeper feeds on insects in crevices in tree bark

Pheasant feeds on seeds, berries and small creatures it finds on the ground

Blackbird turns over leaves in search of insects

Great tit often feeds on the ground

Blue tit feeds at the ends of branches

Sparrowhawk is a day-time hunter specialising in catching small birds on the wing

Great spotted woodpecker feeds on insects and grubs it finds among bark and branches

Marsh tit feeds middle of tree

Jay's food consists mainly of acorns, but it also eats insects, young birds and eggs

Nuthatch feeds on ants and insects in trees

Green woodpecker is often seen feeding on ants in woodland clearings

Birds have adapted in several ways to eat fish. The heron's long bill, neck and legs enable it to wade into deep water to catch fish. The kingfisher dives from a perch and catches small fish in its bill. The streamlined cormorant dives under the surface and catches fish in its long, hooked bill.

Fish-eating birds have dagger-shaped bills, often with a hooked end, but the shapes of the birds vary, depending on how they catch the fish. Both the heron and the kingfisher catch fish, often in the same parts of the river, but the size of the fish caught and the size and shape of the birds are very different. The long-necked, long-legged heron catches its prey by stalking through the shallows, or waiting patiently and absolutely still by the water's edge. The much smaller kingfisher has very short legs because it catches fish by plunging into the water from a perch or after hovering above the surface.

Birds which catch fish by swimming beneath the surface, have webbed feet set towards the back of the body. The body itself is streamlined so they can swim fast underwater. From the illustration here it is very simple to see that the goosander and the shag both share these features and both have thin, hook-tipped bills for catching fish, but they are not members of the same family. Goosanders are ducks, and shags are cormorants. The reason for the similarity is a process known as convergent evolution, which happens when two species that are not closely related evolve in a similar way to make the most of their environment. This often happens even where the species occur in different continents. The birds of Eurasia and Africa are very different species from those in America, but it is often possible to see how one species in the New World has developed in a similar way to an Old World species to which it is not related.

Although only distantly related, the shag (a member of the cormorant family), and the goosander (a fish-eating duck) show similarities in their shapes related to their similar lifestyles. This is known as 'convergent evolution'.

The sea is very rich in food, and birds have adapted to take full advantage of the feeding opportunities.

Gannet feeds on larger fish such as pollack and mackerel, that feed near the surface, catching them in its bill

Arctic tern plunges to the surface to catch small fish and marine creatures

Storm petrel uses its feet to patter along the surface, disturbing plankton and small fish which it then catches in its bill

Guillemot dives from the surface, using its wings to swim underwater for up to a minute, and feeding mainly on small fish found in shoals

Sea-birds nest on land, usually in colonies. Some breed on cliffs while others, such as the terns, prefer flat coastlines. Each species has adapted to make the most of the feeding opportunities by feeding in a certain way and at a certain level. The gannet, for example, feeds by plunging from the sky to catch larger fish that live near the surface. The cormorant, on the other hand, feeds on larger fish near the sea-bed while the similar, but slightly smaller, shag catches smaller fish nearer the surface. With this sort of specialisation there is no competition between similar species and maximum use is made of all food.

Arctic skua chases other seabirds, making them disgorge their food and catching it in mid-air

Cormorant is larger than the shag and its plumage traps very little air, reducing its buoyancy and allowing it to dive deeper and feed on flatfish and other bottom feeders

Fulmar has learned to scavenge on the small fish and offal thrown overboard from fishing boats

Shag is streamlined and underwater uses its large, webbed feet to propel it; it feeds on small fish, such as sand-eels

It is very interesting to examine the way in which birds exploit a particular part of a habitat or ecological niche. Similar species are often found in the same habitat, but they eat slightly different food. In broad-leaved woodland you may find great tits, blue tits and marsh tits, but studies have shown that they all prefer to feed at different levels. The great tit chooses to feed on the ground, in the bushes or the lower branches of the trees; the blue tit, which is the most agile, prefers to search the higher branches for insects; and the marsh tit tends to feed in the tree branches up to about 3 metres.

Much of a bird's life is spent finding food. In fact, often when you are watching birds they are feeding, and there are several ways in which you can discover more about their feeding habits. You may find out what they eat and how each species makes the most of what is available. But remember when you are undertaking any of these projects that you must not unnecessarily disturb the birds you are studying.

Which food is preferred? By a simple experiment you can discover which food garden birds prefer. Take a packet of wild bird mixture and sort out the different seeds, placing each in a separate container. Mark the containers with the names of the seeds or, if you cannot find out the names, use a letter. Place each container in a place where you can watch them and where the birds cannot see you. When you have hidden yourself, record the number of times each species visits a particular container. Put a time limit on the experiment, or record when each container becomes empty.

How much food is eaten? Normally it is difficult to judge how much food a bird takes, but it can be done quite easily in the breeding season by watching adult birds bringing food to the nest. Blue tits and great tits for instance feed their young on caterpillars, and they can be seen entering their nest-holes with bunches of juicy green caterpillars in their bills.

By watching a nest, you can record how many visits the parents make to the nest with food in an hour, and count how many caterpillars they bring each time. By multiplying the number of daylight hours by the number of visits you will discover how busy adults are when they have young to rear. By multiplying the daylight hours by the amount of food brought to the nest in an hour you will find out how much the young eat in a day.

Fish-eating birds are among the birds whose feeding habits are sometimes easy to study. Cormorants, for example, catch fish by diving under water, but they bring them to the surface, which gives you a chance to record how long they stay under water, what sort of fish they catch and how many they catch in a given amount of time.

Herons are rather more difficult to watch, because although they are quite easy to see they move so quickly to grab fish and swallow that you may not be sure whether they have caught anything. However, when a heron has caught a fish, it usually dips its bill in the water, possibly to clean fish slime off it.

Sometimes flocks of birds appear to be doing very little and certainly not feeding. By concentrating on one of the species you can discover when they feed by recording where you see them start, what they are feeding on, and the time of day.

Ducks also show feeding specialisation. There are two main types of duck – the diving ducks and the surface feeders or dabbling ducks. The diving ducks feed by swimming beneath the water in search of small animals, such as freshwater mussels, and underwater plants. The dabblers feed on the surface – just

To find out which type of food birds prefer, you can set up a simple experiment like the one shown here. The method is described in the text.

below it by up-ending, or out of the water by grazing. Shovelers have broad bills through which they take in water. As the water drains out of the sides of the bill, a sieve-like arrangement along the edge of the bill holds back the food that is floating in the water.

The pintail has a much longer neck than the shoveler and this is probably because the pintail is an up-ender, feeding by stretching its neck below the surface. The mallard, which is large with quite a long neck and longish legs, feeds by up-ending, dabbling on the surface and grazing vegetation some distance from the water.

If you look at the identification illustrations in this book (see identification section, beginning on page 112), the shape of the birds will tell you a great deal about their habitats and the way they live.

Inland waters, such as lakes and gravel pits, provide plenty of opportunities for birds to find food.

Shoveler has large bill which it uses to sift the surface of the water for floating food; its bill has a series of filters that allow the water to run out but retain food

Tufted duck is diving duck feeding on small invertebrates beneath the surface

Mute swan feeds from the surface but its very long neck enables it to reach food farther beneath the surface than other surface-feeders

Heron has long legs and long neck, ideal for wading into the shallows to fish

Wigeon has short beak and strong jaws for pulling off leaves, often at some distance from water

Moorhen feeds in the water near the edge as well as wandering into nearby fields in search of food

Mallard can take its food in several ways – directly from the surface, from beneath the surface by up-ending and by grazing on nearby fields

Coot dives for food beneath the surface

Habitats

Although specialisation prevents competition for food and nest-sites between similar species, individuals of the same species still have to compete for food. It is important that they do not compete to the extent that there is not enough to go round.

Territories

To avoid competition, birds set up territories which other individuals of the same species may not enter. There are two main types of territory – non-breeding and breeding. Non-breeding territories may be maintained for feeding and are away from the breeding area. Typical of these are roosting territories and winter territories which are held by some resident species and may not be used for breeding.

Many species do not hold non-breeding territories. Indeed, the most common form of territory is for breeding, but how it is used varies from species to species. Many passerines set up territories that are used for mating, nesting and feeding. The size of these depends on the species. Golden eagles need up to 520 square kilometres while the willow warbler may only need an area not much bigger than the penalty area of a full-sized football pitch.

Some species maintain territories only for nesting and mating, because they have to feed some distance from the nest. This is true of the swallow which nests in barns and sheds, and feeds often some distance away over fields or other open spaces.

Those birds that nest in groups or colonies, such as many sea-birds, maintain a very restricted territory in the immediate area of the nest.

Another form of territory is the mating area. This is temporary and is found among species such as black grouse and ruff, which have gatherings where the males display to each other. The birds that drive off the other males are the ones which hold the territory long enough to mate. This form of display is called lek display.

The purpose of territories is not really known, but scientists have put forward several theories. It is suggested that by establishing a territory a bird provides cover, nesting material and food for its family and protects the family from other males. Territories also spread birds out so that there is no danger of overpopulation. Territorial behaviour helps to strengthen the bond between a pair of birds, and their attachment to the nest-site. In the case of species that rear two broods of young in a summer, the existence of a territory makes remating easier.

Males usually select territories, but what makes them do so or why they choose a particular area is not clear. The urge to set up a territory is thought to be instinctive and the choice of site is probably the result of conditioning. Skylarks choose the flattest possible area, while for cliff-nesting species the choice of site depends on the steepness of the cliffs. For songbirds trees are important.

Some birds can become so conditioned to a particular place that they will continue to nest there long after it has become unsuitable. In the Netherlands, some herring gulls nesting in sand dunes, as they often do, persisted in nesting in the same place even after the dunes had been planted with pines.

Having selected a territory, the male sets about keeping other males out. It does this by attacking intruders, but the attacks are not usually driven home. If they were, both birds might be damaged and the fight would be a waste of time and energy. The attacks, therefore, are ritualised into aggression displays and song, rather in the way that boys stand and threaten each other without coming to blows. It is in fact a war of nerves, with the territory-holder threatening and the intruder escaping when actual confrontation seems likely.

Most birds have particular, threatening calls to warn off other members of the same species, but it is among the passerines that you find the expert singers. Songbirds

Male black grouse displaying at a lek.

The female moorhen invites mating.

establish the borders of their territories by choosing prominent perches, or song-posts, in trees or on fences. The territory extends to within earshot of the song delivered from these posts.

Territorial song

Most species start singing at the end of the winter or early spring when the weather becomes warmer and the hours of sunlight increase. Even when the bird has attracted a mate it continues to sing, both as a warning to other males to keep out and to help cement the pair-bond with its mate.

Like humans, some species have dialects. The chaffinch is a very good example of a species with a basic song, but individuals add new notes. Studies in Scotland have shown that the songs of male birds on one side of a mountain are different from those on the other side of the mountain.

Territorial song must be loud enough to be heard in competition with other singing birds. There must also be variation between species so that individuals can recognise the song of other individuals of the same species. To the human ear the songs of two different species may sound alike, but birds have very acute hearing and they have no difficulty in distinguishing one from another.

Most songbirds sing throughout spring and early summer. After

Above The male approaches. *Below* Mating takes place.

this, it tails off but some species start singing again in autumn. This time their song is not so loud or frequent and is known as sub-song. In a way, it is a form of practice rather like a pianist practising scales.

Courtship

Just as aggression is shown through display and song, so is courtship. The courtship or nuptial display is a ritual which varies between species. They are often similar to aggression displays but the female adopts a submissive posture, crouching with head down and feathers fluffed up.

Part of courtship may be courtship feeding, in which the male (in most cases) feeds the female. The female will beg for food in the same way that young birds do. The male feeds her. Amongst those species that do not form pairs, courtship feeding is most unusual, which suggests that one of the purposes of this ritual is to strengthen the pair-

Courtship of black-headed gulls is a complex ritual.
1 The male shows aggression to establish his territory and frighten off other males.
2 The female places herself alongside the male.
3 A later stage in the ritual.
4 The female takes up a submissive posture.
5 Mating takes place.

bond. In a similar way the birds may indulge in courtship preening. First one, then the other, will preen the head and nape feathers of its mate.

The often complex ritual of courtship reduces the aggression between male and female and is important in cementing the bond between the pair. Mating or copulation usually takes place at the end of the display.

When copulation takes place the male jumps on the back of the female, sometimes hanging on by gripping her neck with his bill. He brings his cloaca, the opening through which the sperm or seed flows, into contact with her cloaca and mating takes place. In some waterbirds there is a *penis*, which only appears outside the body during mating. The species in which it is found are usually those that mate on the water, where there is a risk of the sperm being washed away.

Nest Building

Where a male bird has more than one mate he may be the one to make the nest, but in most species it is the female that does the bulk of the nest-building. Sometimes the female makes the nest on her own, but the males of some species do help the female in the collection of nest material.

Building materials

Bird's nests are extremely varied. They range from non-existent, in the case of some sea-birds that just lay their eggs on a cliff ledge, to the complicated constructions of some passerines. Building materials are often found close to the nest site. Their availability may influence a pair of birds in selecting a particular site. Nest-building sea-birds such as kittiwakes tend to use seaweed and cliff plants for their nests. Grebes use water plants, and ducks which nest on land in long grass use grasses. Although carrion crows usually use sticks for their nests, one pair at London Airport built a massive nest entirely of pieces of wire, which presumably were easier to find than twigs and sticks.

Types of nest

Ground-nesting birds often make little more than a shallow scrape in the soil. An intricately constructed nest would be more likely to attract attention. For protection, the birds

The lapwing's nest is little more than a scrape on the ground.

The great crested grebe's floating nest consists of weeds anchored to plants.

1 The turtle dove builds a shallow, raft-like nest of twigs.
2 Using tiny pieces of mud the house martin builds a nest under the eaves of houses, completely enclosed except for an entrance hole.
3 The reed warbler builds a deep nest of grasses lined with mud.
4 The dome-nest of the long-tailed tit consists of mosses held together with spider's web gossamer, and is lined with up to two thousand feathers.
5 This great spotted woodpecker is cleaning out its nest, chipped out of the trunk of a tree.

must rely on their own camouflage and that of their eggs and chicks.

A contrast from ground-nesting is hole-nesting. Some hole-nesting species search for convenient crevices in trees, cliffs, walls and houses, but others will dig out holes in trees or even long burrows in banks. Best-known of the birds that dig out holes in trees are the woodpeckers. Then there is the little kingfisher which digs out a tunnel with its bill in a steep river bank and nests in a chamber which it builds at the end. The tunnel may be over 60 cm long. The kingfisher's long spear-like, fish-eating bill is an ideal digging tool, especially when compared with the short, wide bill of the sand martin, which also digs out tunnels in steep banks of rivers and sand-pits, but uses its feet to do so. Before starting the tunnel the martin balances itself with one foot, wings and tail and scratches away with the spare foot. Once an entrance is made, the excavation becomes easier because the bird has a perch. The tunnel may be up to 60 cm long.

The really expert nest-builders are the passerines, almost all of which take more trouble than other groups. Crows are passerines and while most species make open nests consisting of large twigs, the magpie puts a roof on its dome-shaped nest, which is made of sticks and lined with fine roots and a covering of mud. Often they make their nests high in trees and build them so well that the strongest March winds seem unable to dislodge them. One nest I know of has not been used for three years and despite its exposed position some 15 metres up in an ash tree, it shows no signs of falling to bits.

Long-tailed tits make complex little ball-nests of moss and feathers, held together with spider's web gossamer. Over two thousand feathers have been found in one nest.

Woven nests are made by house sparrows from straw and dry grass, and lined with feathers. These look untidy but their construction is quite complex. Sparrows are related to the weaver which is found in Africa. One species – the sociable weaver – weaves huge balls of dry grass that hangs from tree branches in which there may be several pairs.

Swallows and martins (except the sand martin), sometimes called hirundines, use mud for their nests. The birds use their bills as shovels, piling up the mud on the top of the upper mandible. The nests are constructed from little pieces of mud stuck together with saliva, but the construction of the nests of each species varies: swallows' nests are cup-shaped with an open top and built on rafters; house martins' nests are built under the eaves of houses with an entrance hole on one side; crag martins have open-topped nests that are built against rock faces; and red-rumped swallows' nests are found on the roofs of

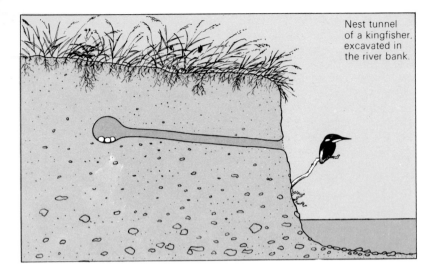

Nest tunnel of a kingfisher, excavated in the river bank.

caves and look like tiny igloos with long entrance passages.

Woodland birds often nest in existing holes in trees, but the woodpeckers dig into the tree trunks to make a nest hole from scratch. The nuthatch, however, reduces the size of the entrance by plastering it up with mud. This behaviour seems to be so instinctive that when nuthatches nest in ready-made nest boxes, they almost always plaster mud around the edge of the hole.

Most familiar of all the types of nest are the cup-shaped nests made by most passerines. These vary from the almost flat nests built by jays and bullfinches to the deep, compact nests of chaffinches and goldfinches. Details of construction vary, even when the nests are made from the same materials; song thrushes and blackbirds both use grass and line the inside of the nest with mud, but the blackbird then puts in a second lining of grasses, while the song thrush leaves the inside of its nest bare.

The nest site

Selection of a nest site is an important business, as important as house-hunting is for people. And while birds may not be too concerned with what the view is like, they are looking for protection from the weather, especially wind and sun. When they are looking for a nest site, birds try out possible places. In the same way that a person buying a bed in a shop lies down on several beds, so tree-nesting species try fitting themselves into forks between the branches and ground-nesting species scoop out a shallow depression in the ground.

Sea-bird colonies often contain several species, each with its own preference for a particular type of site. Shags choose the rock at the foot of cliffs, guillemots the exposed rock ledges, razorbills crevices and the more sheltered parts of cliff faces, kittiwakes the small ledges where the cliffs are steep, and puffins nest in burrows on cliff tops. Herring gulls, lesser black-backed gulls and greater black-backed gulls all prefer the flatter grassy areas beyond the cliff tops and great skuas nest even further from the sea.

Cliffs are the breeding place for a variety of seabirds.

Guillemot nests close together on exposed cliff faces

Cormorant nests low among the rocks at the foot of cliffs

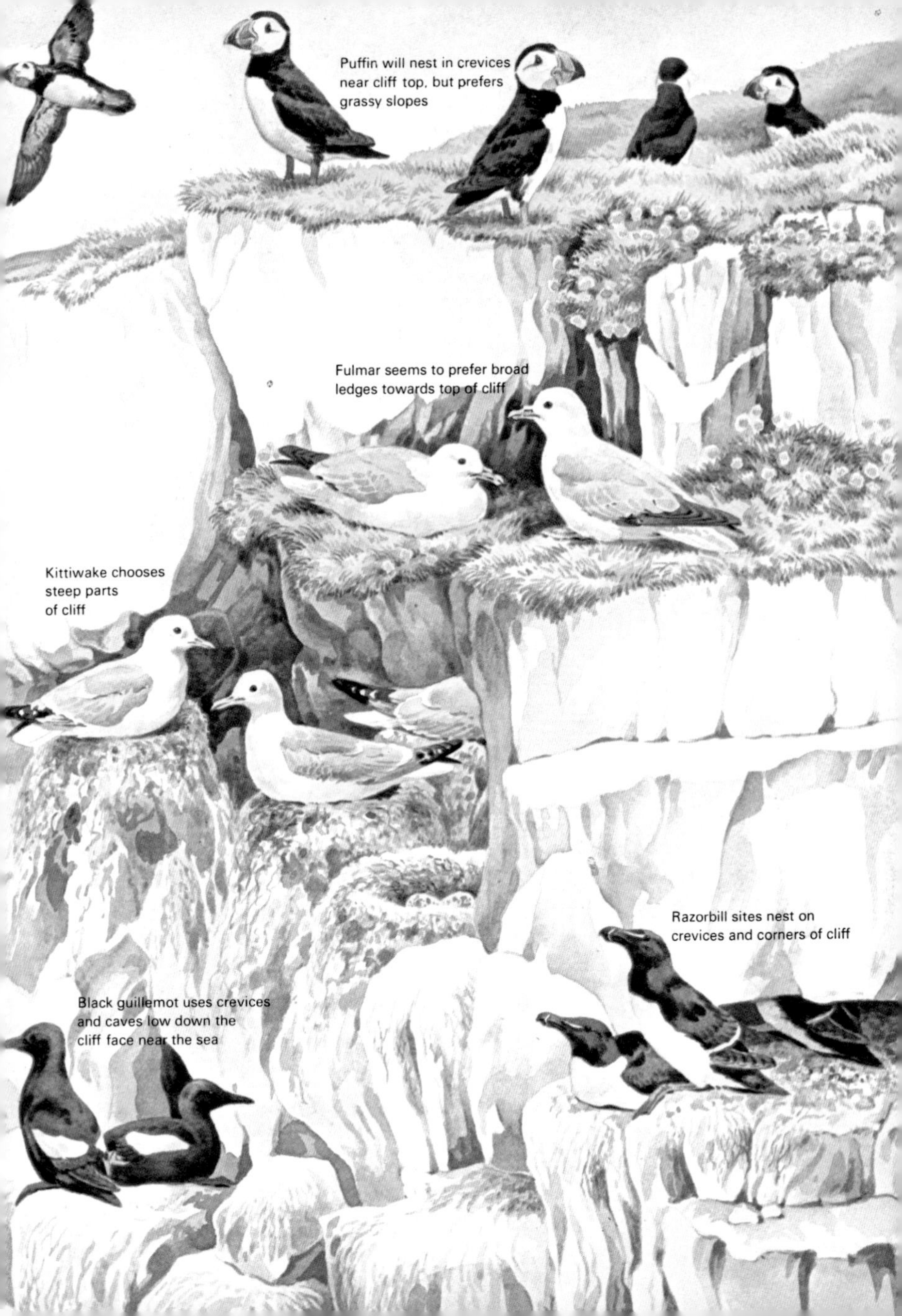

Puffin will nest in crevices
near cliff top, but prefers
grassy slopes

Fulmar seems to prefer broad
ledges towards top of cliff

Kittiwake chooses
steep parts
of cliff

Razorbill sites nest on
crevices and corners of cliff

Black guillemot uses crevices
and caves low down the
cliff face near the sea

Site selection usually follows mating. However, in some cases the nest may be built by the male. These are known as cock-nests. The cock of the wren species is known to build nests and show them to the female. The stimulus to build nests may be related to increased sunlight in the spring or to the growth of vegetation. The stage of plant growth is obviously important to species that have a particular preference for one species of plant. Typical of these is the bearded tit which builds its nest in reeds.

Collecting nest materials

Materials needed for building the nest are often collected from some distance. Usually they are carried in the bill, but many species of birds of prey that build nests carry sticks in their feet.

Nest construction

Although we have very nimble fingers, able to undertake such delicate tasks as threading needles, doing up buttons and making models, without tools we could not match the intricate work of constructing a nest. The intricacy of a bird's nest is even more amazing when you consider that the bird must use its bill, feet and body to hold the material.

Passerines, which are the real expert nest-builders, sit in the cup and build around their bodies.

Bearded tits need to build their nests in reeds of the correct age.

Pieces of grass are pulled over the rim, tucked against the breast, looped over the supporting branch and drawn into the nest. Small pieces are jabbed into the structure with the bill. The shape is formed by the bird fluffing up its feathers and pressing outward with the wings and down with the feet. Nests have to be round to give them strength; if they were oval the tension on them would be uneven and they would be weaker. You can demonstrate this by taking a strip of card 4 cm deep and making it into a circle, and then comparing it with a similar card made into an oval. Under pressure, the oval will become misshapen sooner than the circle. To maintain the shape of the nest the bird continually changes its position as it builds.

Although the desire to make a nest is instinctive, birds learn how to do it by trial and error. Practice in nest-building makes perfect and the longer a bird lives, the better its nests become.

Which of the pair builds the nest depends on the species. As we have seen, male wrens build nests, but in many species the work is left completely to the females. In some, the male assists the female by bringing in material. This may take the form of a display, which presumably helps to maintain the pair-bond. Sometimes, although the male does not help he remains in the territory to protect it.

It is extremely difficult to discover how long it takes a bird to build a nest, because the birdwatcher is often not aware that a nest is being built until its construction is well advanced. The first sign of nest-building is birds carrying material in their bills, but if the birds have only just started, the investigation of the nest-site could cause them to desert. It seems that most passerines take from three to six days. Dr David Lack, whose study of robins over thirty years ago is a classic piece of research into a single species, stated that they took four days working for a few hours each day.

Nesting habits

Long-living species, such as large birds of prey, frequently use the same nest year after year, repairing each season so that it becomes bigger and bigger. The famous ospreys on the RSPB (Royal Society for the Protection of Birds) reserve at Loch Garten have used the same nesting tree since they first returned to breed in Scotland in the 1950s. The birds which now nest there are not the same individuals, but because the place of one of the original pair, which had disappeared, has been taken by another bird the nest site has become traditional. Records show that some sites of golden eagles and peregrines have been occupied for many generations of birds.

Use of old nests

There are opportunist species that make use of other birds' old nests. Kestrels, for example, use old crows' nests, and the disused nests of woodpeckers are readily taken over by woodland hole-nesters such as starlings, jackdaws, stock doves and little owls.

Brood parasites

Most opportunist of them all must be the cuckoo. It does not bother with taking over an old, disused nest – it lays its eggs in other birds' nests. Birds that do this are known as brood parasites and, although in Europe it is only the cuckoo and the great spotted cuckoo that are brood parasites, several other families in the rest of the world have parasitic members – honeyguides in Africa and cowbirds in America being notable species. Individual cuckoos specialise in choosing nests of particular species. More than fifty hosts have been recorded, but some of them may have been used by accident. The most common hosts are the meadow pipit, dunnock, reed warbler, pied wagtail, robin, and sedge warbler.

The cuckoo visits the nest, removes one egg and lays in its place another. The egg that the cuckoo lays looks very similar to its host's eggs, which is why individuals specialise in one species only. The cuckoo's egg usually hatches first and the young cuckoo which is yet unable to see heaves the other eggs out of the nest, using its back which is curved inward for this purpose. The foster parents then bring up the cuckoo which rapidly becomes much larger than its hosts.

Without giving much thought to the cuckoo's behaviour, one may feel that it seems unfair and cruel. But one must consider it not from the human point of view, but from the bird's. Birds are motivated by instincts to breed and rear young. The cuckoo, like all other birds, has no conception of cruelty and the

Female cuckoo approaches a reed warbler's nest and removes one egg.

Having removed the egg, the cuckoo often eats it and then sits on the nest and lays its own egg.

foster parents have no conception of love for their offspring. It seems appalling that the foster parents have to feed a young cuckoo so much larger than themselves, and young cuckoos do appear to be very demanding. But do they eat any more than four young meadow pipits or are they any more demanding than four young pied wagtails?

Top The young cuckoo hatches within twelve and a half days and, using its specially dished spine, it pushes each of the foster-parents eggs out of the nest.
Above After 20 days, when it is just about to leave the nest, the young cuckoo is much larger than its foster parents.
Right Fledgling cuckoo.

Raising a Family

Breeding is timed to coincide with the season at which there is most food available, and when the weather is at its best.

Egg-laying

As soon as the nest is complete the egg-laying begins. In many species, the eggs are laid at intervals of one day, usually early in the morning, but there may be longer intervals between laying amongst larger birds.

Not all species lay the same size of clutch, as the final number of eggs in the nest is called. Guillemots lay one egg in a summer, but the partridge may lay clutches of up to twenty-three. Even among a single species the size of the clutch will vary from season to season or even from place to place. If there is plenty of food available the number of eggs laid will increase. The snowy owl, which breeds in northern Europe, Russia, Canada and Iceland, has many variations in clutch size. In years when the small sub-arctic rodents called lemmings are especially plentiful, the snowy owl lays large clutches and up to four-teen eggs have been recorded. In Iceland, on the other hand, where there are no lemmings and the owls must live on birds, the average clutch size is only four. Similar variations exist with other species.

Sometimes, exceptionally large clutches will be the result of two females laying in the same nest.

How do the birds know when to stop laying? They cannot count, so they are not able to think: 'I've laid six eggs. That's enough. I'll stop now.' The truth is that no one is really sure how they know when to stop. It seems fairly certain that the clutch size is controlled by reaction within the bird's body to an outside stimulus, such as sunshine or other weather conditions.

After the busy nest-building period, egg-laying is a rather leis-urely time for the female. Having laid an egg early in the morning she can spend the rest of the day feed-ing, preening and resting, to build herself up for incubation and the frantic feeding of young. At this time the male is nearby and the pair copulate frequently.

Incubation

In order to hatch, the eggs must be kept warm and it is the parents that do this by sitting on the eggs. This is known as incubation.

During incubation the bird trans-fers body heat to the eggs. To make this easier, the female of many species has brood-patches, which are areas on the underside of the body where no feathers grow and where the skin is thickened with

The greeting ritual of gannets is a prelude to copulation and egg-laying.

blood vessels that transfer heat to the eggs. Not all species have brood-patches; one that does not is the gannet, which uses its huge feet to transfer body heat to the eggs.

Males which share the incubation with their mates have brood-patches too. Among the passerines, those males that do not incubate have no brood-patches. The amount of incubation done by either sex varies between species. Most usual is incubation by the female alone. You can often tell which sex does the incubating by its colouring. It is important that an incubating bird is well camouflaged, unless it is a hole-nester. Therefore, where the female has more drab colouring than the male,

it is likely that she alone incubates. Typical of these species are the mallard, pheasant and chaffinch.

Where the male alone incubates, he tends to be less colourful than the female. This happens with the dotterel, a plover that nests on high moorland, and with the red-necked phalarope, a small wading bird.

Sometimes males and females share the incubation equally, or the male just helps out occasionally. Often, although he does no incubation, the male stays near the nest and feeds the female. Where the pair share the work, they will often go through a greeting display when they change over.

The point at which the bird starts to incubate depends on the species.

In most passerines it starts when the last egg has been laid. Some species may start incubating when the last egg has still to be laid. Others, notably many birds of prey, start to incubate with the first egg. This is called synchronous incubation and means that in a large clutch the last chick to hatch may be a couple of weeks younger than the first to hatch. Although the youngest chicks may die because they are unable to compete with their brothers and sisters for food, such spaced out hatching helps to ensure that the eldest do survive, and gives the youngest a chance if the food supply holds out.

Grebes, which build huge, untidy nests of water-weeds, cover up the eggs with pieces of weed when they leave the nest. It is thought that one of the reasons for this is to protect them from other birds that might eat the eggs. When they are laid they are chalky white, but they become stained green or brown.

Protecting the eggs

Eggs are a source of food for many predators and therefore a number of methods of protection have been developed. The eggs themselves are often camouflaged, especially those that are laid by ground-nesting species. The parents, too, are camouflaged and when a predator is close the incubating parent sits tight, only moving at the last moment. If the incubation has only just begun, the parent is more likely to leave the nest when threatened. As it progresses it sits tighter. In the

Woodcock nest among bracken in woodlands. Their delicate pattern and colouring make them very difficult to see, especially if they sit motionless.

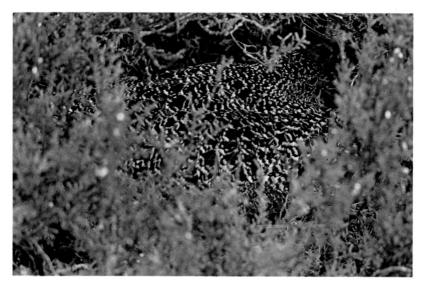

Above The red grouse has cryptic plumage to conceal it when nesting on heath or moorland.

Below left Lapwing eggs and chicks blend in with their surroundings.
Below right The bold markings of the little ringed plover nesting among pebbles on the seashore disrupt the bird's outline, making it extremely difficult to spot. The eggs themselves are camouflaged and look very similar to stones, as do the young.

early stages of incubation the parents may desert the nest altogether if disturbed.

The birdwatcher and nesting birds

Nesting birds should be disturbed as little as possible. A good birdwatcher never disturbs them. If you approach a nest and there is a bird sitting, you should leave immediately. And never stare the bird in the eye because this is just what predatory mammals do when they are stalking their prey. If you stare at the bird you will make it leave the nest and possibly desert it altogether.

The touch of your hand on the eggs will not cause the bird to desert, because the sense of smell of a bird is not very well developed. However, there is a risk that your presence may make the bird desert or may attract the attention of predators, particularly members of the crow family. Generally, therefore, you should keep away from nests.

Length of incubation

The length of the incubation depends on the species. Albatrosses and kiwis may take up to eighty days while small passerines may only need ten days. Among European birds the longest incubators are sea-birds, with the manx shearwater taking up to fifty-four days, and large birds of prey, with the griffon vulture taking fifty-five days.

Why should there be such differences in length of incubation between species? All sorts of theories have been put forward – the size of the bird or its eggs, the length of life of the bird, climate, food supply, time of year and how developed the chick is when it hatches, have all been suggested. The reason is probably a combination of several of these. The species whose chicks are well developed when they come out of the nest are often those that take longer to incubate.

Development at hatching time

Young birds emerge from the egg in various stages of development, ranging from the blind, helpless, naked young of passerines to the down-covered, sighted young of the megapodes which are entirely able to look after themselves. Megapodes, which are game-birds from South-east Asia and Australasia, bury their eggs in holes, cover them with vegetation that rots and heats up like a compost heap and then leave them to hatch; the young are able to look after themselves when they hatch. Amongst European birds the most advanced young are those of the ducks and waders. On hatching they are feathered and can see and feed themselves, but they follow their parents on whom they are dependent for warmth and protection, particularly at night.

Some stages in the development of the egg.

At 72 hours, the main blood vessels are visible. The enlarged front region is due to the fast development of the brain and eyes.

At 5 days, the embryo is lying on its side, and one eye and a rudimentary limb can be seen.

At 7 days, the head forms half the body size. Note the attachment to the yolk sac. Development continues steadily until the time for hatching.

Others, for example partridges, follow their parents but are unable to find their own food. The parents do not actually feed their young but they do show them the food. Moorhens and coots, although they are active and can walk and swim, need to be fed by their parents.

All these birds are precocial, which means that they are down-covered, have their eyes open and leave the nest soon after hatching. Species which leave the nest at this time are called nidifugous species.

Nidicolous species are those that remain in the nest after hatching. Some, such as gulls, are feather-covered when they hatch and can see, but they do not leave the nest until they are able to walk. These birds are described as semi-precocial. Then there are chicks which are down-covered but are unable to leave the nest. These semi-altricial species, for instance the heron family and birds of prey, may hatch with their eyes open or, as in the case of owls, they may be blind on hatching.

The perching birds and some other land birds are described as altricial. The chicks are blind, have little or no down and are fed by their parents. They rely on their parents for food and warmth.

Young birds defined

You will find that young birds are described in several ways. Often, terms are used incorrectly, but any-

From egg to maturity.

Egg

Just hatched

Fourteen days (just out of nest)

Late summer

one who wants to become a good birdwatcher should try to use the right words to describe young birds. Scientists use the word 'pullus' (or pulli if there is more than one) for a bird until it is full-grown and able to fly. At this stage the terms 'nestling' and 'chick' are also used. The next stage is when the young bird has its first real feathers or juvenile plumage. Exactly when a bird changes from juvenile to immature is not well-defined and the word immature is used usually for those species that take several years to reach maturity. Small perching birds develop very quickly into adults, while for large birds of prey and seabirds, it takes several years before they are mature enough to breed.

Feeding and care of the young

Once the young have hatched, the parents are kept very busy providing food, especially among nidicolous species. You will notice, during the breeding season, garden birds searching furiously for food and flying back to their nests with bills full of food for their young. Food-carrying is a sure sign that the adult has young in the nest.

Most passerine parents share the feeding and many take turns at brooding the young to keep them warm. This also happens with birds of prey whose chicks may hatch over a period of several days. When the male takes over the brooding

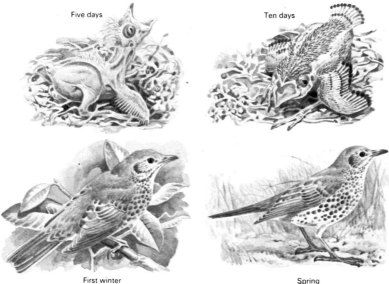

Five days

Ten days

First winter

Spring

from the female he may deliberately push the eggs that have not yet hatched to the back of the nest, because he does not incubate eggs.

Nestlings have very large mouths or gapes. The open gape stimulates the parent to fill it with food. Sometimes a parent will be carrying food to its own nest and spot a fledgling of another species. So strong is the stimulus of the gape that it may feed the fledgling rather than its own young.

Another strong instinct in nesting passerines is the need to remove droppings from the nest. The droppings of the young are produced in tiny transparent bags called faecal sacs, which means that they can be removed easily in the bill of the adult.

Growth of the young

Growth of the young once they have hatched is rapid. The linnet, a small finch, incubates for ten to twelve days and feeds its young in the nest for eleven to twelve days. When the young can fly and leave the nest they are said to have fledged. So, fledging in linnets takes no more than twenty-four days from the start of incubation. Larger birds take longer; the gannet, for example, incubates for about forty-four days and it takes another ninety days for the young to fledge.

The linnet lays between four and six eggs and usually rears two or even three broods in a summer, but the gannet lays only one egg and does not have the time to rear more than one chick in a year. The linnet reaches maturity, and can breed, in the summer after the year in which it was reared, while the gannet does not reach breeding maturity until its sixth year.

Survival rate

Only the fittest birds survive until the next breeding season and despite the larger number of eggs laid by some species, the survival rate is low. Small birds have a very short life expectancy in their first year – on average no more than nine months. If they manage to live more than nine months their life expectancy increases to a year and it remains at a year from then on. The average life expectancy of a songbird is between one and two years.

More deaths occur among the young birds whose experience is not very great and which are in danger from such predators as cats and birds of prey, or are unable to find enough food. The mortality rate is highest among the immature birds, but once a large bird has reached maturity its chances of survival are good. Gannets, for instance, may live up to forty years.

Ringing

Studies of the ages of birds have been greatly helped by the introduction of ringing. Ringing is a method of marking birds by fixing a very light metal or plastic ring to their leg. The first ringing experiments were carried out in Great Britain in 1890, but these were very limited. It was a Dane, Christian

The aggression display of this grasshopper warbler is used to frighten off intruders.

The distraction display is intended to lure intruders away from the nest.

Mortensen, who undertook the world's first major ringing scheme in 1899. Germany, Hungary, Great Britain, Yugoslavia, the Netherlands, Sweden and Norway had all begun effective schemes by the First World War. After that war, the rest of Europe, Japan, Canada and the United States also introduced ringing schemes.

Ringing is now extensive in northern European countries and has given us a great deal of information about weights and movements of birds. After the Second World War several schemes for ringing sea-birds were introduced and some fulmars ringed as adults in the late 1940s were found to be still alive in the mid-1970s. Professor Dunnet, who still catches fulmars he ringed in the 1940s, has pointed out that the birds show far less outward signs of ageing than people.

Regulating the population

The study of the way birds regulate their populations is a complex one, known as population dynamics. Birds do manage to regulate their numbers, but the number of young produced does not seem to be the main factor in keeping the population stable. This suggests that the controlling factor must be the number of birds that die. The three most likely causes of death are disease, predation by other animals and starvation due to lack of food. When numbers become too high it is a combination of these causes that reduces the population to the level where there is enough food and space to support it.

Protecting the young

To protect their young some birds attack. Blackbirds, for example, will strenuously attack marauding jays. Others will try to draw away a potential predator. This is called a distraction display. Usually the parent pretends to be injured in the hope of attracting the predator away from its young. Mallard make an alarm call that sends the ducklings swimming for cover, and then splash around in the water, gradually moving further off and drawing attention away from the young.

If you see a bird putting on a distraction display, keep your distance and allow it to get back to its young. Another problem you may find is that nestlings that are about to fledge all jump from a nest if disturbed. It is possible to collect these and place them back in the nest with your hand over the top. The darkness will quieten them down and they should stay in the nest. However, young birds have enough dangers to face without human interference, so avoid peering into nests.

This lesser whitethroat is helping to keep the nest clean by picking lice from the underside of the nest.

This female redpoll is shading her nestlings from the sun's glare by spreading her wings.

Above Another form of sanitation is shown by the lesser whitethroat removing a faecal pellet from the nest.
Left A grasshopper warbler sheltering its young during a rain storm.
Below The moorhen chick instinctively follows the parent's flicking tail.

Bird Movements

Very few birds stay in one place throughout the year. Some places just do not have enough food to support a varied bird population at certain times of year and only a few species can remain. This happens on moorlands and mountains; only a few species such as ptarmigan and red grouse can spend the winter on the snow-covered ground. Other birds move into lowland areas and some even fly thousands of kilometres for the winter.

Sedentary species

Birds that do not move very far over the year are described as sedentary. One of the very few species that does not move far from the area where it hatched is the wren. In the British Isles the robin is mainly sedentary, but in Scandinavia and northern Germany it moves south in autumn. British robins are known for the way in which they trust man, but Scandinavian robins breed deep in woodland, keeping well away from man. It is thought that the Scandinavian robin's distrust of man comes from having to face the barrage of guns and nets of the so-called sportsmen of northern Italy, when they migrate south in autumn.

Although British species such as the robin, song thrush and wood pigeon do not move very far from one place, there are some European races of robins, song thrushes and wood pigeons which are seen in winter, especially on the eastern side of the British Isles when they are moving south-eastwards.

Short-distance migrants

Everyone knows that the cuckoo and swallow winter in Africa and move north in winter to breed in Europe. They are called long-distance migrants, but many species move shorter distances at various seasons of the year, or even daily. Starlings, for instance, move out of towns to feed in the country each day and many great tits move from the woods, where they breed, into gardens in towns in autumn.

Cause of bird movements

All these movements, whether they be seasonal or daily, are caused by environmental conditions, usually connected with food and roosting places. If you live in a city you may have noticed that at certain times of day you see large flocks of starlings. At daybreak in winter, flocks of starlings will fly out of the town into the countryside to search for food. In the evening they fly back to roost in the town. Some country starlings roost in flocks in trees and range out many kilometres to find food.

Many of the wood pigeons seen in Britain in the winter are migrants from Europe.

Gulls, many of which come inland in winter, roost in flocks on open spaces such as playing fields. Each day they move off, searching for food in rubbish tips or where fields are being ploughed. Greylag and pink-footed geese feed on farmland in small flocks. The flocks come together each evening to roost on the water of lakes. In Scotland, on a late afternoon in winter, you can see flocks of grey geese flying in to roost on lochs, having spent the day feeding on farmland.

Seasonal migration

Seasonal migration takes place in spring and autumn. Spring migration is generally northward or north-eastwards to breeding grounds, and in autumn the migration is generally southwards or south-westwards. Migration is caused by different factors among different species, but generally it is related to the abundance of food. Swallows, for example, feed on small flying insects and if you look, you will not find many flying insects before April when the swallows arrive from the south. Likewise, when the swallows have left in early autumn you will find that the flying insects on which they depend for food have also disappeared.

In most of Europe we have a two-way migration, with winter visitors that breed in the far north, sometimes within the Arctic Circle, arriving just after the summer visitors have flown to the south. Some birds stay throughout the winter, but others stop on their way even further south. These birds are known as passage migrants.

The time of day when a bird migrates depends on the particular species. Geese, ducks and gulls will travel by day or night. Herons, storks, crows, eagles and hawks are daytime travellers, while most passerines travel by night. The night-time migration of small birds is significant in giving them the cover of darkness in their travels, and daylight during which to feed. Waders are dependent on tides, so that they move when the tide is high and their feeding grounds are covered, whether it be day or night. Swallows and martins, which catch insects as they fly, do not need to stop in order to feed and so they travel during the day.

Old wives' tales suggest that birds can forecast weather and that a large number of winter migrants means a hard winter. This is nonsense. A large number of winter migrants means that there has been a good summer and that many birds which might have otherwise starved have survived. Weather can have a serious effect on migration. Bad weather may prevent migration from starting or halt it before the birds arrive at their destination. This may account for migrants arriving late, but taken over the years the arrival dates have been remarkably regular. Clouds affect the height at which the birds migrate; when there is cloud cover birds usually fly above it. During the day most birds fly up to about 1,000 metres and at night at 1,500 metres, but waders will travel at about 6,300 metres.

Long-distance migration

Many birds travel very long distances. Swallows travel over 10,000 kilometres from Europe to South Africa, but the real marathon bird is the Arctic tern. This seabird, smaller than a black-headed gull, breeds in Europe right up into the Arctic and each autumn migrates south to the Antarctic. Some Arctic terns do a round trip of more than 30,000 kilometres a year and thus enjoy more daylight than any other animal, the Arctic in summer having twenty-four hours of daylight and the Antarctic in winter having the same.

To most of us who rely on signposts and maps for moving from one place to another, the ability of birds to travel long distances and not get lost is a miracle. How they manage it has puzzled scientists for many years. Experiments with manx shearwaters showed that this species can find its way home even from an area that it does not normally visit. One of these birds was taken from the island of Skokholm, off the west coast of Wales, to Boston on the east coast of the USA. The bird returned to its burrow on Skokholm in twelve and a half days, having made a journey of 4,000 kilometres. And it had never made this journey before.

Navigation

How do birds find their way? It

seems from experiments that they almost certainly use the position of the stars and sun to navigate by. Migrant birds in captivity have shown restlessness and an urge to move in the direction in which they would migrate if wild. Other experiments using artificial suns and depriving the birds of sunlight have reinforced the theories that navigation by sun and stars is used. It is not known how the birds relate the position of the sun or stars in the sky to direction-finding.

Hazards

Sudden storms and cloud may make the birds lose their way. This accounts for sudden falls of migrants where they are not usually seen and for sea-birds suddenly appearing inland when they are almost always seen at sea. Species which only turn up accidentally like this are known as accidentals or vagrants. Migration is a very dangerous business for birds. Large areas of water may have to be crossed, but wherever possible birds choose migration routes over land, crossing seas at the narrowest points. There are three main migration routes across Europe. The largest water mass that migrants from Europe must face is the Mediterranean Sea. To do this they use the shortest sea crossings – the Straits of Gibraltar between Spain and North Africa, from the foot of Italy through Sicily to North Africa and down the east of the Mediterranean.

Desert is another hazard for migrants to Africa and when they reach Africa they have to face a journey of more than 1,900 kilometres over the Sahara, where there is very little food or water. Unfortunately, the farming to the south of the Sahara is reducing the natural vegetation and the desert is spreading south. This

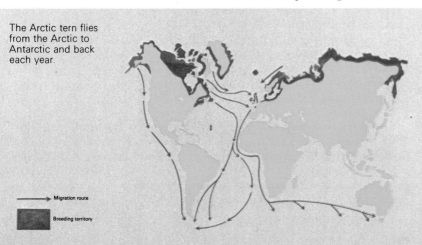

The Arctic tern flies from the Arctic to Antarctic and back each year.

Migration route

Breeding territory

is making the migration even more hazardous for birds.

Lack of cover is another migration hazard. When they reach land after crossing the sea or when they have crossed a desert, birds often need to feed and rest. Without cover they cannot do this in safety.

Weather is probably the greatest hazard that migrating birds must face. As we have seen, the sudden appearance of cloud can cause birds to lose their way. Storms when the birds are on the wing can be lethal. A small bird, such as a starling, stands very little chance if a storm comes up as it is crossing the North Sea. The wind and rain force it down towards the surface and the nearer the surface, the greater the risk of it being swamped by waves.

Considering all these dangers, it is hardly surprising that so many birds fail to live more than nine months. But on top of all the natural hazards man has added his own. Lighthouses attract migrants with their powerful lamps, and many of them smash into the lights and are killed. Our need for electric power means that our countries are crossed by gigantic power lines, into which birds fly, so breaking their necks. Another hazard has arisen in the shape of the huge flares which occur when excess gas is burned off in the North Sea oilfields. Some ornithologists are worried that these flares might attract migrating birds which would be burnt in the flames. Finally, there is in southern Europe the widespread and inexcusable trapping of birds as they migrate. In northern Italy many migrants from Scandinavia, Germany and the Netherlands are shot or trapped as they arrive, having just crossed the Alps. The trapping methods are often inhumane; one of them uses captive birds to call down the migrants to waiting shotguns, nets, traps or sticks covered with a sticky glue-like substance, known as bird-lime. When a bird lands on a twig covered in bird-lime its feet stick and as it struggles, its feathers become coated with the substance. There is not enough evidence to be sure whether the number of birds killed reduces the breeding population of a species. Certainly, many people feel great disgust at the cruelty of this 'sport', however.

Travelling in flocks

Many birds travel in flocks. Some nest in colonies and move around in flocks in winter, while others nest individually in pairs but form into flocks outside the breeding season.

The flock has two main values. Firstly, it gives added protection against predators because there are more pairs of eyes to keep watch for danger. Something approaching a flock of birds may be noticed by one of its number, which will call as it takes off. The immediate reaction of the other birds to the alarm call is to take off too. This is obviously an advantage against ground pre-

The main migration routes of birds of prey across Europe.

dators such as foxes, but flying flocks are also in danger from birds of prey. Sparrowhawks and peregrines will visit roosting sites of starlings each evening as they come in to roost. In these cases, to be in a flock is a disadvantage to the birds that are caught, but the species as a whole is at an advantage because it is the weaker fliers and less wary birds that are caught. The survival of the species is then helped because it is the fittest birds that survive.

The second value of the flock is the ease of food-finding. With so many pairs of eyes in a flock searching for food, there is a greater chance of food being found. Another advantage of the flock is that males and females can pair up before the flock disperses, allowing more time for the setting up of territories and for nest-selection.

Birds in flocks, especially when flying at night, rely on calls to maintain contact. These are invaluable to the birdwatcher, because it is almost impossible to see flying birds at night. However, one can identify the birds passing overhead by listening to their call notes. During the day this is a useful way of sorting out flocks of birds when the species look similar in flight.

Man & Birds

Birds were living on this planet long before man came along. From the moment he arrived things began to change for birds. He soon discovered that birds' eggs were a useful source of food. Then he perfected the sling, the bow and arrow and traps and he began to hunt the birds themselves. However, it is unlikely that he made much difference to bird populations through his hunting; he was just another predator alongside birds of prey, owls, foxes and other carnivorous mammals.

The changes became more pronounced, for birds and for other animals, when man turned from a hunter into a farmer. He began to fell forests to make way for his fields of corn. Then he started to domesticate cattle, sheep, goats and pigs, and they needed grazing land. Indeed, as man became civilised, so the face of the world began to change.

However, the major changes have come in the last two hundred years. Farming methods became more specialised and efficient, machines were introduced into industry and the population grew rapidly so that more houses were required. Even so, in Europe the changes were gradual compared with those wrought by European man when he settled in other continents.

The extinction of the great auk was due to man's ruthless hunting, both for food and for superstitious reasons. The last great auk was killed in 1844.

Extinction of birds

Of the 129 species of bird that have become extinct since 1600, the only European ones were the great auk, a large, flightless north Atlantic seabird, and the Cyprus dipper. It is significant that they were both island species; of the species in the world that have suffered extinction, all but about ten have been island species.

Destruction of habitats

Man's main effect on birds has been through the destruction of their habitats. Forests have been cut down to provide land for farming and the farm animals have grazed the natural vegetation. When civilised man travelled and settled abroad he took with him sheep and goats which have had a disastrous effect on the native vegetation and, consequently, on the native fauna that relied on it. Unwittingly, he also took rats which proved lethal to some species of bird, especially flightless island ones. The homesick settler introduced European bird species too, and some of them competed with, and took over from, native species.

As well as chopping down forests, man has also drained marshes and lakes. His effect on the wetlands has been even more dramatic and damaging than it has on woodland. Now it is vital that every effort be made to maintain the wetlands that still exist, for many of the species of birds that are found in wetlands are unable to adapt to new habitats.

Man's population growth

In recent years, with the growth of population more land has been swallowed up for industrial development. This is because an increasing population demands more manufactured goods, more roads, more airports and so on. Although in recent years, people have become more aware of the need to protect our environment, conservationists still have to fight very hard to persuade planners and governments

The effects of oil pollution are only too obvious on this guillemot.

A skylark in a bird-trapping net in south-west France.

that we must use our natural resources wisely.

Pollution

Industrialisation has caused pollution. The most obvious form of pollution is by oil, and it is common on a trip to the seaside to come across oil on the beach. These sticky lumps are simply annoying to people when they cling to the feet or clothes. But to birds, oil pollution probably means death – a slow uncomfortable death from cold, poisoning or drowning. Unpleasant as this is, the worst aspect is that oil pollution is not selective and any species of sea-bird is at risk. The wreck of a supertanker or a blow-out in the North Sea oilfields, could have devastating effects on northern European sea-bird colonies. This is particularly worrying as most of the world's populations of razorbills and gannets breed on northern European coasts.

Chemical pollution is not as obvious as oil because it does not appear in great black slicks. An oiled bird is easily detected, but a bird that has died from suspected chemical pollution has to be examined internally. Fortunately, this form of pollution appears to be diminishing, but in the twenty-five years after the Second World War it had serious effects on birds. Chemicals called organo-chlorines were developed as insecticides to kill insect pests, and herbicides to kill plant pests, and were used extensively in farming. Ornithologists then began to discover large numbers of dead birds in farming areas and began to find the cause.

The birds worst hit were the predators because the chemicals went up through the food web. Insects containing both the insecticides and seeds dressed with herbicides were eaten by songbirds, which were then caught by birds of prey. While the doses of chemicals in the songbirds were not always enough to kill them, their bodies retained the chemicals which then became lodged in the birds of prey. So, the doses would build up sufficiently to kill the predator. Sometimes the dose taken by the predator was not enough to kill, but enough to make it sterile or to make eggshells so thin that they broke before they hatched.

Fortunately, these chemicals are used much less now, and this is largely due to the quick rection of conservationists and the pressure that they brought to bear on the agro-chemical industry and governments. The populations of birds of prey were dramatically reduced by persistent chemicals but it now seems that they are beginning to increase their numbers.

There is another type of pollution which is more worrying to anglers than to bird-watchers, but which can affect birds. It is pollution of water by fertilizers. The fertilizer is spread over fields and is then washed by rain into ditches, streams, ponds and rivers. The fertilizer works just as well on water-plants as it does on crops, causing them to grow so fast that they take nearly all the oxygen in the water, not leaving enough for the fish and insects that live in it. Without fish and insects the water-birds have nothing to feed on.

Other threats

The destruction of habitats and pol-
lution are indirect threats to birds, but man can also threaten birds more directly through activities such as shooting, trapping and egg-collecting. Although, in themselves, these activities are usually not enough to endanger a species, they can have a serious effect when the species is otherwise threatened.

Shooting, when controlled by traditional rules of behaviour, with closed seasons during which it is illegal to kill birds, does not usually have any adverse effects on the populations of individual species. However, indiscriminate shooting can be very serious and for this reason most European countries have passed laws to protect at least rarer birds.

Trapping birds for food and for cages still happens in most of Europe, but on a large scale in the Mediterranean countries. It is unselective, with rare as well as common birds being caught. In addition, it causes unnecessary suffering to the birds caught.

Deliberate poisoning of crows and birds of prey seems to be increasing, especially in hill-farming areas and where game is preserved. The method used is to treat the corpse of a rabbit with poison or to inject poison into chickens' eggs. The bait is then left in a place where it is likely to be found by crows, buzzards or eagles. In most countries this is illegal, because the poisoned bait is dangerous to domestic animals as well as birds and other wildlife. Baiting is usually done through ignorance; birds of prey are often, wrongly, held responsible for the death of game-birds and livestock such as sheep and lambs. Hatred of any birds with a hooked bill and talons used to be widespread among gamekeepers, but fortunately many are now much more understanding towards them.

Egg-collecting is another very selfish human activity for which there is no defence. Egg-collectors are strange people who seem to get a thrill from stealing the eggs of rare birds. This can prevent rare birds from increasing their ranges and can be fatal to species that are diminishing.

Bird conservation

With birds exposed to so many different threats, it is important that there are some people who are concerned for their welfare. These people, the conservationists, fight to protect birds in several ways. They are not just protesters; they take positive action by providing reserves where birds can breed or shelter in peace. Merely taking an area of land, putting a fence round it and putting up a sign saying 'Nature Reserve' is not enough. The land has to be managed to make the most of the available habitats – for instance, the vegetation may be controlled so that one particular plant does not overwhelm the area.

Reeds on wetland reserves are prevented from spreading and destroying meres, while on woodland reserves young birch trees are cleared to give undergrowth a chance to grow.

Research is important to the success of conservation projects. Without certain information the management of reserves would be impossible; the conservationists would be unable to recognise such dangers as pollution, or to take action against them. It is also important to be able to inform people about birds, whether particular species are harmful or not to man's activities, and how the damage they do can be minimised.

In the last twenty-five years, conservationists have achieved an enormous amount in changing public opinion about birds and the need for their protection. They have prevented development schemes that would have done irreparable damage to birds. And they have shown that through co-operation with government and industry a great deal can be done to improve our environment without harming man's development.

Conservationists will always have a lot of work to do, and anyone who is interested in birds should give his utmost support to the bird conservation organisations in his country. The main conservation body in the United Kingdom is the Royal Society for the Protection of Birds.

Equipment for Birdwatching

People can go birdwatching any-where. Look out of any window and you are likely to see a bird. Most people watch birds at some time in their lives, even if they are only the familiar ducks and swans on the local pond or river. But serious birdwatching requires preparation and quite a bit of action.

How do you start? What equip-ment do you need? You will get by with nothing more than a notebook and pencil at first, in fact.

Notebooks

Notebooks come in many shapes and sizes and what you choose depends on what is convenient for you. You will certainly not need a large notebook for use in the field. In fact, you want one which will fit into your pocket, and a good size is about 10 cm × 15 cm. It needs to be hard-covered and the pages should be ruled. To stop the pages flapping about in a breeze it is useful to stretch a thick rubber band round the front cover and the pages you have already used. This means you can immediately turn to the page you want. It is also useful for hold-ing your pencil.

Pencils are much better than pens for use in the field, because they do not run out at awkward moments. And if they break they can be sharpened. Personally, I pre-fer to use a short pencil because it is easier to handle. Make sure that you use a brightly coloured one, not green or brown, so that you can rec-ognize it if you drop it in the under-growth

Armed with a notebook, sharp pencil and pencil-sharpener, or a penknife, you are all set for bird-watching. You can start to make notes of what you see – the physical characteristics of birds and their behaviour.

Keeping notes

Making field-notes about birds that are unfamiliar is the best way to identify them. All notes should show the date, place and time. Then you should include as much infor-mation about the bird as you can – size, colouring, shape, how it flies, its song, what it is doing. On page 92 are field-notes of three common species. See if you can identify them from the notes. Use the iden-tification section, beginning on page 112 of this book, to help you.

All the birds described below were seen within ten minutes on the edge of a school playing field on the 2nd May 1977.

1 About sparrow-size. Black head, rosy red breast, grey back, white rump, black tail. Stocky shape and thick bill. Dipping flight with white wing-bars showing on black wings. Flew along hedge.

2 Two birds. Smaller than sparrow. Collecting grass on ground (nest material). Red on face, yellow on wings. Brown bodies. Flew up to tree, showing yellow wing-bars in flight. High pitched call.

3 Flying bird. Sparrow-sized. Heavy body with short tail showing some yellow. Light not good enough to see colour of body but it appeared dark rather than light. Dipping flight. Wings longish and broad where they met body.

These birds may seem easy to identify, but there are occasions when field-notes are invaluable in identifying unusual species. Some rare birds are unmistakable, but to sort out migrant waders from North America or divers and grebes in winter plumage, there is no good alternative to notes. If you rely on your memory and look up details of description in a book when you get home, you will not be sure of the identification. You will find yourself trying to remember whether the legs extended beyond the tail in flight or whether the bill turned upwards. An identification book can be a hindrance when you are watching birds, because you may not have time to look up the correct pages. It is much easier to write down what you see and check it with books later. Even if your drawing is not very good, it is worth doing a rough sketch and marking the areas of colour and other features on it. Some rough outlines are shown here.

An example of field-notes.

Field-notes are very important for recording behaviour. Trying to remember later what a bird has been doing is very difficult.

Knowing how much to record in your notes is difficult at first. However, after a time you will be able to judge quite quickly what to put in or leave out. At first it is best to record everything you can – weather conditions, time of day, type of habitat, how long you watch for and how long particular movements of the birds take, the number of birds present, and so on. One should also note whether whatever was happening appeared to end naturally, or whether it was stopped by an outside influence.

Weather conditions may be very important factors. Rain or wind are thought to affect behaviour in a number of ways. There are some interesting questions that one may ask: does bad weather prevent birds from feeding? Does wind direction affect the direction in which flocks of birds travel? Does courtship display only take place in certain conditions? How soon after it has been raining do birds start singing again?

Time of day may have a significant influence on bird behaviour. Do birds feed more at certain times? During the breeding season, do different sexes feed at different times of day? Again, you must remember before you draw conclusions that you perhaps watch birds at particular times of day.

Notes on the type of habitat in which you are observing a bird can give you a lot of information about its behaviour. A species that finds itself in a foreign habitat will often behave in a most interesting way.

Observation of the number of birds present in feeding and courtship situations can yield some useful information, too. For instance, when observing the courtship of the house sparrow, you will see that although several males are involved, only one actually copulates.

A time-piece

A watch is a useful item of equipment for the birdwatcher. The best type is a stopwatch, but for most of us an accurate watch with a second hand is good enough.

Binoculars

Sooner or later, if you are serious about birdwatching, you will want a pair of binoculars; it will probably be sooner. You can watch birds without binoculars – indeed, it is very good practice to do so, because you soon learn to recognise species at a distance by their shape or behaviour – but you can do so much more with binoculars.

Nowadays there is a bewildering selection of binoculars for sale and choosing a pair for yourself can be very difficult. For most of us, the main consideration in making the final choice is the cost. Good quality binoculars are very expensive but many cheap pairs can be found and are quite good. When buying, you should test several different models. It is best to try them out in natural

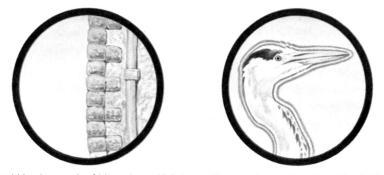

Avoid buying a pair of binoculars which have either bending at the edge of the field of view (left) or colour fringing (right).

light, through an open window or outside the shop.

At the eyepiece end of the binoculars will usually be two figures joined by a multiplication sign – for instance, 8 × 40. The first figure is the number of times that the binoculars multiply the image of the object you are looking at – in other words, the magnification. The second figure is the diameter, in millimetres, of the objective lens. This is quite as important as the magnification, because it affects the light-gathering property of the glasses. Dividing the objective lens diameter by the magnification, will give you the exit pupil diameter which indicates the light-gathering power. This is important especially for birdwatching in woodland, twilight or bad weather. The higher the exit pupil diameter, the less chance you will have of straining your eyes when using the binoculars. The exit pupil diameter of 8 × 40 binoculars is 5, and anything below 5 is not really adequate for birdwatching. Below is a list of exit pupil diameters for the most common types of binocular.

6 × 30	**5**	9 × 45	**5**
7 × 50	**7**	10 × 50	**5**
8 × 30	**3·75**	11 × 60	**5·4**
8 × 40	**5**	12 × 60	**5**
9 × 35	**2·9**		

From these figures, you can see which binoculars have the best light-gathering properties. It is certainly not worth sacrificing good light-gathering for higher magnification. Generally, the higher the magnification the smaller the field of view, and the smaller the field of view the more difficult it is to find with your binoculars a bird that you have seen with the naked eye. Some, described as 'wide angle', do increase the field of view. If you go to a reputable dealer he will be able to advise you about the fields of view of most makes of binoculars, because the manufacturers usually supply this information. Another disadvantage of high magnification is that the higher the magnification the further away is the minimum focusing distance. An 8 × magnification enables you to focus on objects 4 or 5 metres away; with a 7 × you can focus on objects even nearer.

The magnification you need depends on the places where you go to birdwatch. For general birdwatching the best are 7 × and 8 ×; anything larger is not suitable in very close country such as woodland, because you need to be able to focus at quite short distances, and light-gathering is important. However, for birdwatching in open country, on estuaries or very large stretches of water, the higher magnifications are better – 10 ×, 11 × or even 12 ×. But, remember that lower magnifications are still quite good in open country and unless you can afford the extra money, it is not worth buying another pair of binoculars.

Your arms can become very tired when holding binoculars to the eyes for a long spell and their weight can make them bear down on your neck. So while a heavy pair of naval binoculars may look very attractive in a shop, they will almost certainly be a nuisance on a long field-trip, and it is much better to buy a lighter pair. Also, make sure that they are comfortable to handle, that you can reach the focusing wheel with ease and that your hands do not shake when holding them. If they do, and the ends of the binoculars move, the shake will be magnified as many times as the magnification of the binoculars. Some manufacturers are making binoculars with zoom focusing, so that by simply pulling a lever you can alter the focus very quickly. I find them hard to handle and the optical quality generally inferior to that of conventional ones.

You may wonder how you can judge the quality of binoculars. Testing them before you buy will give you some idea. Compare several different makes for the sharpness of the image they give. Watch out for colour fringing, a term used for the colour outline which can appear around the image, and for distortion of the object at the edge. You can test this by focusing on a straight line, such as a flagpole or the side of a building; if the line is not straight then the binoculars must have an aberration.

Telescopes

Telescopes are used by some birdwatchers, especially those watching migrating birds or sea-birds. Their magnification of up to 60 × is invaluable in identifying birds a long way out to sea or sorting out birds of prey on migration. A telescope is much more difficult to use than binoculars and the problem of a shaky hand is greatly magnified. A tripod is therefore needed.

Clothing & Fieldcraft

The clothes you wear for bird-watching must be really comfortable and protect you from the weather. It is unpleasant to feel uncomfortable when you are bird-watching. For this reason the ideal clothes for colder weather are warm and waterproof, but light. A light-weight but warm anorak or water-proof jacket is very important, but make sure that it is made of material that doesn't rustle.

Clothes for camouflage

Birds do not trust people and you must make yourself as inconspicuous as possible when you are watching them. One of the ways of doing this is to choose clothes that are well-camouflaged. Bird-watchers have learned a great deal from birds about how to camouflage themselves. The best jackets to wear are the combat jackets which are patterned with several shades of green and brown. They should also be silent jackets – many modern man-made fabrics rustle when you move, and birds have excellent hearing. Jackets or anoraks with hoods are useful because they break up the outline of the head and shoulders. A hat with a brim, has the same effect, the best sort being the bush-hat. However, in the winter you will need a woolly hat to keep your head warm. It won't

break up the outline of your head but you can solve this problem by pulling your hood up over the top.

Choosing a jacket

Remember, when buying a jacket or anorak, to make sure it has plenty of pockets, which you will need to carry equipment such as your note-book, and any interesting things you may find on the way.

Out in the field

Now, fully equipped, you are ready to go out into the field in search of birds. You will soon learn that birds are wary creatures, so you will need to employ fieldcraft. This is an invaluable skill to the birdwatcher and to be good at it you must understand how birds react to people.

Birds have an instinctive distrust of all other animals until they learn that there is nothing to worry about. Unfortunately, man has done little to encourage the trust of birds, and in most cases they will be hostile towards you. So you must try and get as close to them as you can without them realising.

The secret is to use cover and move quietly. Cover is anything you can hide behind, such as a hedge, a tree-trunk, a parked tractor or a wall. Look round the sides of cover, rather than over the top. If you look over the top of a hedge, for instance, your head will be outlined against the sky, but if you look round the end of it or, better still, through it you will stand less chance of being seen.

The ground that is sheltered behind cover is called dead ground. Small hills and ridges may provide dead ground, for example, and you may be able to use it to approach birds more closely. It may be further to go but you are likely to have better views than you would have if you approached directly. Moving quietly in the countryside is more important than moving quickly.

Where cover is low you should keep below it. The best ways to advance are by edging along the ground on your stomach or running on all fours.

You must always be watchful for obstacles like overhanging branches or puddles. While it is uncomfortable to walk into such obstacles, it is also noisy, and noise must be kept to a minimum.

When you are with other bird-watchers, you should restrict conversation and use signs to communicate wherever possible. But do not wave your arms around too much, because you will be very conspicuous. Noise problems can arise in a group of birdwatchers when one person cannot see a bird and needs another member of the group to point it out to him. In these cases, you should use the clock method to point the bird out. Taking an easily recognisable landmark such as a tree or large rock as the centre of an imaginary clock, refer to the position of the bird in terms of a line

Always look round cover; never over it

Finding birds by the clock method of direction. The bird marked here is at 2 o'clock from right-hand top corner of front barn.

drawn through one of the figures round the edge of the clock. Thus the instruction, 'From top of left hand end of gate, partridge at two o'clock,' would mean that to see the partridge you would have to look along a line running from the top of the gatepost to the figure two on your imaginary clock.

Binoculars in the field, can be a nuisance at times, especially when you are moving. They tend to swing about and, if you jump across a ditch, are quite likely to fly forward and fall back, hitting you on the chest as you land. There are two things you can do about this – tie a knot in the strap to shorten it and make sure that you hold the binoculars against your chest if you move fast.

Although birdwatching can be a fascinating and exciting hobby, it may be dangerous and you must never let your enthusiasm take over from your good sense. It is not worth injuring yourself for the sake of seeing a bird. In fact, there have been several fatal accidents, with birdwatchers falling over cliffs or becoming stranded by the tide on estuaries. So do not take silly and unnecessary risks or fool about in dangerous places, such as cliff tops or mud-flats.

For birdwatchers, as for anyone who goes walking in the country-side, maps are important. Using a reliable, detailed map, such as one of the Ordnance Survey 1:25000 Series, you will be able to plan your birdwatching trips to take in the most likely looking areas. And you can ensure that you don't get lost!

In some parts of Europe, bird-watchers have a very bad reputa-tion among farmers, other land-owners and even wardens of nature reserves. This is because a few birdwatchers, in their enthusiasm, have carelessly walked through standing crops and left gates to fields open. These people, although in a minority, have done much harm to the general reputation of birdwatchers. So, do remember to obtain permission before going on to private land and avoid causing damage to crops or farm animals.

Finally, no birdwatcher can hope to become good in the field unless he remembers that the welfare of the birds he is watching must come first.

Tracks & Signs

Not all species of birds are easy to watch, but there are other ways of learning about them. It is surprising how much you can find out from the tracks and signs that they leave.

Footprints of birds

Birds do not leave such obvious tracks as mammals, but you can find their footprints in wet mud or sand and in the snow.

Making casts of prints

An interesting and informative collection of casts of footprints can be made. Having found a firm, well-defined print, all you need to make a cast is plaster of Paris, which can be bought at most chemists, a jug of water, a strip of metal foil (cooking foil will do) or stiff card, and a stick or a wooden spoon. First, fold the strip of foil to form a round or square frame, whichever fits the shape of the print best. Place the frame around the print. Mix the plaster of Paris and the water in the jug stirring with the stick, and allow it to stand for a couple of minutes. Then pour the mixture slowly into the print, making sure that you do not damage the outline and that the mixture spreads right through the shape. After a quarter of an hour or so the cast should set.

While you are waiting for the cast to set, note details of the time, place, date and other interesting points such as the type of ground in which the print was found and how far apart each print was. When you get home with the cast, you can make a positive impression on another cast. First smear it with vaseline, covering every part of the top surface. Then place another foil frame on top of the greasy cast and pour on more plaster of Paris. When the positive cast is dry you can paint it, using a pale shade for the surface and picking out the impression in a darker shade of the same colour. Store your collection of casts in boxes.

Making plaster casts. The method is described in the text.

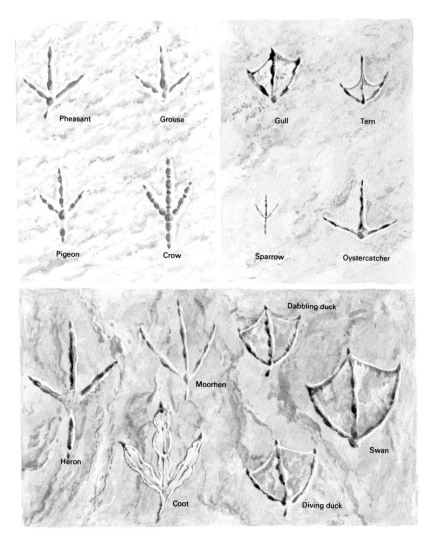

Common bird tracks to look out for. N B. These are not to scale.

Other signs to look for

There are several other signs to look for which can tell you much about a bird's presence. Most of them are concerned with food.

Carcases

The carcases of birds and mammals will give clues to the identity of their predators. Sometimes it is difficult to tell whether the carcase has been left by a bird of prey or a mammal, such as a fox, because carcases do not lie around for very long, and several different animals may feed on them.

Another reason why few carcases are found is that the birds of prey often take their prey to a plucking post. In the breeding season they use plucking posts all over the territory, but outside the breeding season they are more likely to use one favourite post. They can be recognised by the mass of feathers scattered around them.

The larger the prey the more likely it is that there will be some remains. But these do not usually last long. In Spain and eastern Europe, farm animals, particularly sheep and cattle, may die and attract the attention of the specialist carrion-eaters. First to find the corpse will be the magpies, whose bills are not specially adapted for tearing flesh, and they will prod the soft parts. Soon, other scavengers will be attracted – the large griffon and black vultures which tear at the flesh; the small Egyptian vulture whose thinner, hooked bill is perfectly adapted to reaching the pieces that the larger vultures miss and probing for the bone marrow; and black and red kites which grab the pieces of flesh left by the others.

Shrike's larder.

After a couple of hours there is little left but some scattered bones.

Small birds of prey such as owls and kestrels that feed on small rodents swallow them whole and do not leave any remains.

Larders

Shrikes are small passerines that feed on large insects, lizards and small rodents. They take their prey to thorny bushes or barbed wire, where they impale them on the thorns or barbs for later use. The collections of food are known as larders and during the breeding season are a sign that a nest is near. Shrike larders are very difficult to find because they are often deep under cover, and not all shrikes have them.

Egg-shells

Eggs of birds are often eaten by

101

other animals, including birds. The remains of egg-shells can often give a clue to the identity of the animal that has been eating them. Not all the egg-shells that you find will be the remains of another animal's meal. Egg-shells of nidifugous species usually remain in the nest until the young leave, but they are then carefully removed some distance away from the nest. If they were left lying near the nest they might be a clue to a predator that there was a nest nearby with eggs in it. You can usually tell whether eggs have hatched because the lining extends beyond the edge of the shell and folds inwards. The egg-shell will be quite empty. Eggs eaten by other birds will usually have traces

The remains of food can be a useful clue to the presence of a particular species.

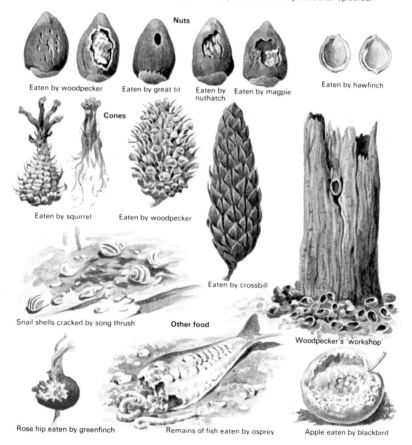

Nuts

Eaten by woodpecker   Eaten by great tit   Eaten by nuthatch   Eaten by magpie   Eaten by hawfinch

Cones

Eaten by squirrel   Eaten by woodpecker

Eaten by crossbill

Woodpecker's 'workshop'

Snail shells cracked by song thrush   **Other food**

Rose hip eaten by greenfinch   Remains of fish eaten by osprey   Apple eaten by blackbird

102

of blood or yolk in them. Gulls and crows steal eggs and usually make a large irregular-shaped hole in the egg-shell. Mammalian egg-stealers like rats and foxes usually break the shells more thoroughly than birds.

Song thrushes leave traces of their food when they feed on snails. The thrush usually uses a favourite stone, brick, tree stump or even a square of concrete to smash the shells on. A collection of smashed snail-shells around a stone is a sure sign of the presence of a song thrush.

Holes in ant-hills

If you find an ant-hill with holes dug in it, you can fairly safely assume that it is the work of a green woodpecker. Smaller holes in large numbers may be the work of flocks of starlings. Holes on the seashore made by waders are usually accompanied by footprints. Bee or wasp nests are dug out by honey buzzards, which take the combs away to their nests to feed their young. Badgers are also known to dig them out.

Vegetable remains

Vegetable remains can be clues to the presence of birds. But you must remember that rodents, too, eat seeds, nuts and fruits so it is worth learning the different ways in which mammals and birds tackle these foods. Often, birds attack fruit or cones of conifers when they are still on the tree, but so do rodents, such as the wood mouse, which is a good climber. However, rodents use their front teeth or incisors in such a way that they usually leave toothmarks, while birds must use their bills to pierce or crack the food.

Nuts and cones

Woodpeckers and nuthatches often wedge nuts and cones into crevices in treebark to hold them steady while they strike them with their bills. Nuthatches choose smaller nuts, and the holes which they make are smaller than those made by woodpeckers. In woodland where there are trees with deeply creviced bark, it is always worth keeping an eye open for nutshells wedged in trees. Woodpeckers have favourite spots where they open nuts and cones, and these will be heaped at the foot of the tree.

Hazelnuts, which have very hard shells, are eaten by several species of birds and mammals. The mammals attack with their teeth, leaving fairly neat holes in the shells, but birds pierce with their bills, leaving ragged holes, sometimes surrounded by bill marks. The nutcracker splits the nuts in two. The smaller cherry stones are treated the same way by hawfinches, which use their powerful jaws to split them in two. Hawfinches are rather shy birds and scattered halves of cherry stones are one of the most obvious signs of their presence.

Fruit

Windfall fruit in autumn is eaten by rodents and birds. Sometimes the same apple or pear will be eaten by both. The birds that are very partial to fruit are thrushes, blackbirds and starlings, all of which have relatively thin bills. Their bills enable them to jab at the fruit leaving the flesh covered in tiny lumps, while rodents gnaw with their front teeth and as a result leave regular marks.

Pellets

Much of the food that birds eat contains hard material that cannot be digested. Bones, fur, feathers, husks of seeds and the hard parts of insects, which are made of a substance called chitin, have to be disposed of because the bird cannot always digest them. Therefore, the bird gets rid of them by bringing them up through its beak. All the indigestible parts of the food build up in the bird's gizzard, which is in the front of the stomach. They are pressed together to form a hard lump or pellet, which is covered with a liquid produced in the stomach called mucus. The mucus acts as a lubricant which helps the pellet's passage up through the body.

Equipment for dissecting pellets.

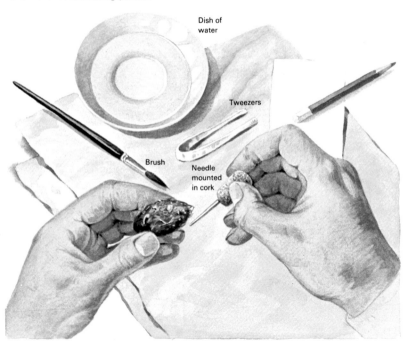

Dish of water

Tweezers

Brush

Needle mounted in cork

The size of the pellet depends on the size of the bird's throat and is an important factor in identification. It is thought by many people that pellets come only from birds of prey, but in fact a lot of species produce them. Small birds produce small pellets which are often overlooked.

Birds of prey usually produce cylindrical pellets, while in the case of some species of gulls and waders, the shape may be spherical. Some typical pellets are illustrated here.

By dissecting pellets you can find

Pellets are the undigested remains of a bird's meals, and are useful for telling what the bird was feeding on. Many birds can also be identified by their droppings or faeces. N.B These are not to scale.

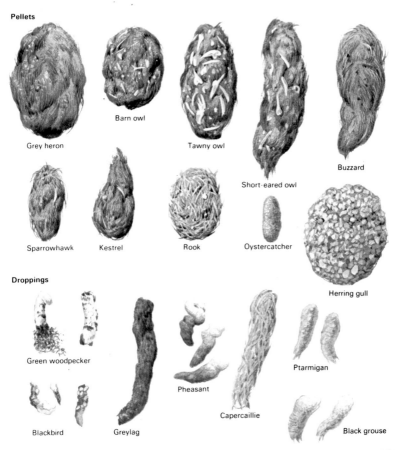

Pellets

Grey heron

Barn owl

Tawny owl

Buzzard

Short-eared owl

Sparrowhawk   Kestrel   Rook   Oystercatcher

Herring gull

Droppings

Green woodpecker

Pheasant

Ptarmigan

Blackbird   Greylag

Capercaillie

Black grouse

out a great deal about the food of birds. When you find a pellet, note when and where and the type of habitat. Good places for finding pellets are nest sites, roosts, plucking posts and feeding sites. If you know what species are using these sites you can probably identify the pellet. If not, take measurements, draw a sketch and write a description before you start to analyse the contents. You can then use this to compare with any further pellets you find.

To do this, you need a dish of warm water, two large darning needles, tweezers or forceps, a soft paintbrush and blotting paper. Soak the pellet in the water for half an hour and then gently tease it apart with the needles. Remove bones and insect remains, brush them clean with the soft paintbrush and wash them, leaving them to dry on the blotting paper.

Now comes the interesting part. A birdwatcher comes to learn about many animals other than birds because he has to identify bones of small mammals, and parts of insects, fish and reptiles. Your local library will probably have some books that you will find useful for identification, and some helpful suggestions are given on page 185.

Even if you are unable to identify the complete contents of the pellet, you should mount all the material on a piece of strong card. Beside each piece that you have identified, write its name and include details of

where and when the pellet was found. Later, as you learn more, you may be able to identify some of the unknown pieces.

Droppings

You will have noticed that birds have droppings. These can be almost as useful to you as pellets when you are seeking information about birds. Mammals produce urine and faeces separately, but in birds they are mixed. The urine is usually white and the faeces are dark brown. The presence of droppings on tree branches, cliff faces or at the entrance of holes in trees are clues to the presence of birds. Often, by looking for droppings, you can tell whether a hole-nest is being used.

Some droppings will tell you what a bird has been eating. In late summer and autumn when there are blackberries and elderberries, the droppings of thrushes, blackbirds and starlings may be pinkish, mauve or even purple. Woodpeckers produce cylindrical droppings, rather like the ash on a cigarette and containing the chitin from ants. Gamebirds produce firm droppings and the droppings of the capercaillie, measured over a day, will amount to a metre in length. Geese and swans also produce large droppings and the regular roosting site of a family of mute swans will be covered with greenish droppings up to 16 cm long.

Records & Surveys

The importance of keeping notes when you are birdwatching has been stressed in the last few pages, but it is also vital that what is written down can be read at a later date. Unless you are able to write very neat field-notes that you will be able to read in a few years' time, it is worth re-writing the rough notes you have made when you get home. In this way you can keep an orderly record of your observations, which will be easy to refer to at any future date.

Arranging your notes

To do this properly you need to adopt a methodical approach. Unless you are careful, notes can become so complicated that you give up in despair and do not bother any further. You could arrange your notes under several headings, such as places, species or even behaviour, but this is not very satisfactory. For instance, you would find it difficult to look up information about a particular place when your records are arranged under species.

Therefore, the best thing to do is to make a fair copy of your notes in a hard-covered notebook and number the pages. You can then make a card index, keeping details of species, behaviour, places, and so on, in alphabetical order with page numbers. Number the book itself so that when it is filled up you can start your second book. References can then be noted with the book and page number. The entries in your index could appear like this:

Great crested grebe, courtship display – Book 1 p.22

House martin, arrival dates – Book 1 p.10, Book 2 p.8, Book 3 p.12

Morecambe Bay – Book 1 p.56, Book 2 pp.2, 45, 64

Listing species

The simplest way of recording is to make a list of the species you see. Many types of list can be kept – life lists, place lists, holiday lists. These can be great fun to make, but they do not really provide very much information.

One form of listing, however, can provide interesting results. It is to keep a daily tally of the species seen in a certain place. This can be done on your journeys to and from school, in your garden or on holiday. You can use squared paper with the names of the birds listed down the left-hand margin and the dates across the top of the page. This sort of record is particularly interesting over several years, because you can compare one year with another.

Recording dates

Recording the dates on which you first see migrants can be interesting when you compare different years. A survey carried out by birdwatchers in America showed that all the migrants arrived at weekends. Since birds have no conception of days of the week this seemed very interesting, until someone realised that it was at weekends that the birdwatchers did their birdwatching; many of the migrants had no doubt arrived during the week but were not spotted until the weekend. This demonstrates a phenomenon known as observer bias, something that you must be wary of when you are drawing conclusions.

Observing feeding habits

Studies of birds' feeding habits can be very rewarding and although much scientific research has been undertaken there is still a lot to be learned. You can do a simple experiment in your own garden by putting out dishes of different foods for the birds. All sorts of edible material may be used, but it might be a good idea to start with seeds of several kinds – maize, millet, barley and oats. Record the species that visit each dish and how many visits are made over a certain period of time. (This experiment is described in more detail, and illustrated, on pages 48 and 49.)

A study of water-birds will yield valuable information about feeding. The best place to study them is a lake or gravel-pit. Draw a map of the area, including the land around the edges, and mark where the birds are feeding. From this you will build up a clear picture of the different species' preferred feeding places. You can also record the ways in which they feed – sifting through food on the surface, up-ending, diving beneath the surface or grazing at the edge.

Make a study of the time that diving birds stay beneath the surface. This is fascinating because if you can see what they bring to the surface you can get an idea of how deep they dive. For instance, if you see a cormorant coming to the surface with a flounder then you can assume that it has dived to the sea-bed.

A survey of breeding birds

Breeding birds give plenty of scope for surveys. By mapping where you see birds singing you can plot their territories. You can also keep records of the dates on which you see birds beginning to nest, when you see them carrying food and when you see young birds around. It is also interesting to observe the positions of the nests themselves. Do hole-nesting species choose holes that are facing in certain directions? Do they avoid holes facing in one particular direction?

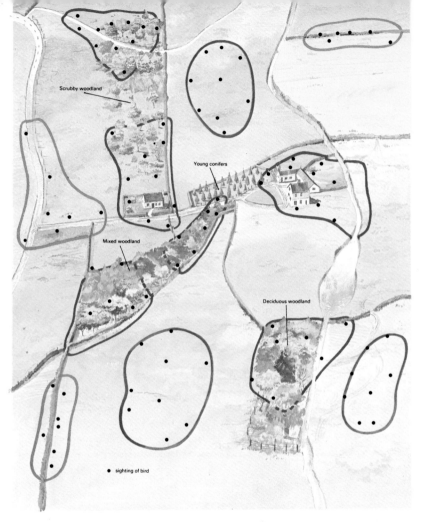

You can plot the breeding territories of birds in your area on a map. This example shows the territories of blackbirds (red), yellowhammers (orange) and skylarks (blue).

Using maps

Maps are very useful to the bird-watcher. Most useful for surveys covering a small area are maps of the Ordnance Survey 1:25000 Series. These show all the main features of the landscape quite clearly. They can be purchased from many bookshops, if not directly then by order.

Collecting

Nowadays, no serious birdwatcher collects eggs. Egg-collecting is a very thoughtless action and illegal throughout most of Europe now. Nesting birds have enough dangers to face without the further threat of ignorant and stupid people stealing eggs. However, as you will have noted from previous chapters, there are other things connected with birds that you can collect.

Wings and feathers

Attractive displays can be made from the wings and feathers of birds. They should be cleaned of any remaining skin or muscle by rubbing them with a solution of borax or salt and water.

When setting wings, allow one to dry in a folded position but spread the other as it would be in flight. Spread it face down on a piece of soft board and use steel pins to hold it open. It should set in a week and can then be removed from the board.

Wings can be mounted in several ways. One of the best is to sew the wing gently to a piece of stiff white cardboard with loops of appropriately coloured cotton.

When you have removed any flesh or skin from the feathers you can glue them on a piece of thick

Wings and feathers can be cleaned and mounted on card to make attractive displays.

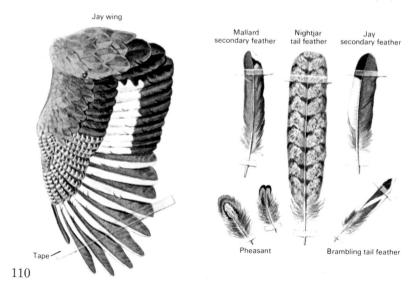

Jay wing

Tape

Mallard secondary feather

Nightjar tail feather

Jay secondary feather

Pheasant

Brambling tail feather

white paper or mount them loosely by making cuts in the paper, as our illustration shows. Both wings and feathers should be stored in boxes containing moth-balls.

Nests

It is illegal to collect nests when they are being used, but it is permissible to collect them during the winter when the birds are not breeding. To be sure that you are not disturbing any birds, the best time to collect nests is between October and January. Do not collect nests of species that return to the same site each year – namely, herons, corvids, birds of prey and house martins. To be safe, it is best to avoid taking any nest measuring over 30 cm in diameter. Sometimes, old nests are used by other animals for shelters, and they should not be touched; mice and even toads have been known to hibernate in them.

Because they are fragile, nests must be handled with the greatest care. To move a cup-shaped nest, fill it with cotton-wool while it is still in place in the habitat. Stretch string around the nest to hold the cotton-wool and nest in place, so preserving the shape while you take it home. Dry the nest out, remove the cotton-wool and string, then pack it in a box with new cotton-wool. Write a label for the box listing details of the species, place and date collected.

Taking a nest apart can tell you a

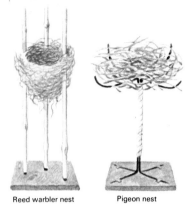

Reed warbler nest   Pigeon nest

Old nests can be mounted on simple frames to make attractive displays.

lot about its construction. It will also make you marvel at the amount of material that birds collect to make their nests. To unravel a nest you need to take a lot of care and have very agile fingers. First, write down the depth and diameter outside and inside the nest and note the place where it was found, including the height from the ground. Then you can start unravelling.

Pile the contents in heaps of similar material – mud, twigs, pieces of grass, rootlets, moss, feathers, hair and leaves. Then note down how much of each there is. The mud and moss can be weighed and twigs, grasses and rootlets measured. The leaves and feathers can be counted and identified, if possible. Having done this, you may be able to work out the nearest supplies of all these materials. You may be quite surprised by the results of your research.

Identifying Birds

On the following pages we have tried to show birds as you will see them, describing the characteristics by which you will be able to identify them. But when you see a bird you cannot identify, you will want to know what points you should be looking for. In identification one must ask a series of questions as outlined below, and so, by a process of elimination, find the correct answer.

How big is the bird? By assessing the size of the bird you are watching you will be able to eliminate a large number of possible species. Size is often very difficult to judge, especially at a distance, but if there are other birds present and you know what species they are, you can use them for comparison. If there is no other bird for comparison, and you are unable to judge the size, do not despair, because there are other features that can help you identify the bird.

What is the bird's shape? As described on earlier pages the shapes of bodies, wings, legs and bills differ from one species of bird to another. These variations are associated with the behaviour patterns of species, and they act as very useful recognition clues.

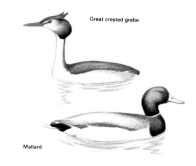

Great crested grebe

Mallard

Notice how different water-birds, such as the great crested grebe and mallard shown here, sit on the water

What are the bird's colouring and patterning? Although colouring can be an aid to identification, it is not the best guide. Firstly, few species have very obvious, bright colours and, secondly, the way a bird's colour appears to a birdwatcher may depend on the light in which he sees it. For example, a house sparrow seen in the light from a brilliant sunset may appear red, and a swan

Size is relative. Black-headed gulls appear small compared to great black-backed gulls, but large when compared to, say, redshank.

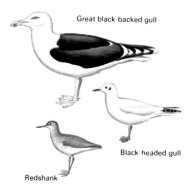

Great black-backed gull

Black-headed gull

Redshank

Use plumage patterns for identification. In flight, these finches all appear very different.

seen against the light may look black. Patterns of plumage, on the other hand, may be excellent clues. Consider such bold body markings as the robin's breast or the white rump and black tail of the bullfinch. Wing patterns can be vital in identifying waders and finches. Remember that all you may see of a bird is the rear view as it flies away. *How does the bird move?* On the ground some species of bird hop, others walk or run and some do all three. Species that feed in trees may move up and down the tree trunks: watch the way they do this? Swimming birds may also give away their identity by the way they move through the water. The moorhen is easy to identify because it moves its head and neck backwards and forwards like a clockwork toy as it swims. Observe how the bird sits in the water – is it riding high with

Look at the way a bird moves through the air. Is the flight deeply undulating as in the woodpecker's (top) or direct and fast like the starlings (bottom)?

plenty of body showing and its tail cocked upwards like a gull's, or is it low in the water like a cormorant?

There are special points to look for when you see a bird in flight. They are the speed of the wing-beats – rapid as in waders or slow and deliberate like herons; the height at which the bird is flying – very high like a feeding swift or low over the fields like a feeding swallow; and the movements of the bird – undulating like the woodpecker's, jerky like the tit's, fast like a goose or hovering like a kestrel.

How does the bird behave? Many species can be differentiated by the way in which they behave. Ducks, for instance, can be divided into those that dabble or feed on the surface and those that dive for their food. Having determined the way in which a duck is feeding, you will be able to cut down the list of possibilities. Feeding behaviour is a good clue and should always be noted.

What is the bird's song like? Among songbirds and waders the noises that a bird makes are often the only indication of its identity. Some birdwatchers claim to be able to distinguish between willow warblers and chiffchaffs by observing the colours of their legs and plumage, but the only sure way of telling them apart in the field is by listening to their song. Learning bird songs and calls is very difficult and it is even harder to note them down. It helps if you have a good ear for music and are able to remember a sequence of sounds. The best way of learning bird songs and calls is by listening to records or cassette recordings.

What is the bird's location? The place where you see the bird will also give you clues to its identity, but you must take into account the time of year. Wheatears, for example, breed in moorland areas but you may see them on migration in lowland farmland. Most birds migrate in spring and autumn and these are particularly exciting seasons for the birdwatcher, because you never know what is going to turn up.

Making field-notes has already been dealt with on pages 91 to 93, but it cannot be stressed too strongly that the best way of identifying a bird is to make notes about it when you see it and check them later with books. Of all naturalists, birdwatchers seem the most concerned to make positive identifications of species. Often, however, positive specific identification is impossible, but you may at least be able to determine the genus or even the family. Do not be ashamed to admit it if you are unable to be specific; many ornithologists are quite happy to use descriptions such as 'willow/chiff' for what might have been a willow warbler or a chiffchaff, or 'comic tern' for an arctic or common tern.

Of course, it is exciting to see a rare bird, but do not be too anxious to persuade yourself that the bird you have seen is a rare species. If

114

you are in doubt about whether you have seen a common or a rather similar rare species, favour the common one – you are more likely to be right.

On the following recognition pages we have not followed any of the accepted scientific orders in which birds are listed. Instead, we have tried to present all the similar species together so that you can compare them.

The areas where the birds are found are named, and if you are in doubt about their exact position, you can look them up on the map on page 178.

The measurement which appears after the name of the bird is the average length from the tip of the bill to the tail.

The capital letters after the measurement refer to the status of each species in the British Isles. They are as follows:

R — resident, present throughout the year
S — summer visitor
W— winter visitor
P — passage migrant occurring on passage in autumn and spring

Some species of birds may fall into more than one of these categories. If there is no initial, it means that the species does not occur in the British Isles.

All birds illustrated in this section are adult, unless otherwise specified as imm. (immature) or juv. (juvenile). Where the sexes are different ♂ denotes male, and ♀ denotes female.

The external features of a bird

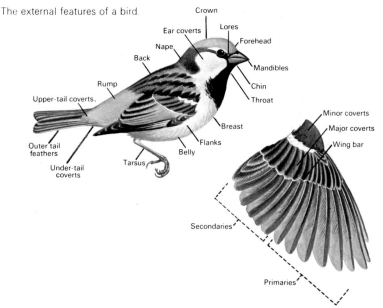

Crown
Ear coverts
Lores
Forehead
Nape
Back
Mandibles
Chin
Throat
Rump
Upper-tail coverts
Minor coverts
Major coverts
Wing bar
Outer tail feathers
Breast
Flanks
Belly
Tarsus
Under-tail coverts
Secondaries
Primaries

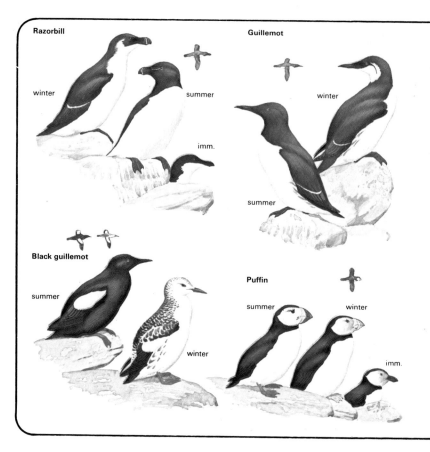

Razorbill *41 cm RS*

Blacker than guillemot and with thicker bill. Often flies over sea in small flocks. Breeds in colonies on sea-cliffs in north-western Europe and winters in north-west Africa.

Guillemot *41 cm RS*

More slender and brown than razorbill, with noticeably thinner bill. Has straighter back when flying. Breeds on colonies on cliff ledges on coasts of north-western Europe, and winters at sea in east Atlantic.

Black guillemot *33 cm R*

Note black plumage with white wing-patch. In winter back and wings much paler than guillemot. Stands less upright than other auks. Flies with very fast wing-beats. Nests on rocky shores in Scotland, northern England and Northern Ireland. Stays close inshore all year.

Puffin *30·5 cm R*

Large head and bill very noticeable, especially in flight. Nests in colonies in cliff-top burrows in north-western Europe.

Sandwich tern *24·5 cm S*

Black bill tipped with yellow, and black legs. Forked tail without streamers and crest-like cap. Wings very pale grey. Nests in colonies on shores and islands in British Isles, Netherlands, Denmark,

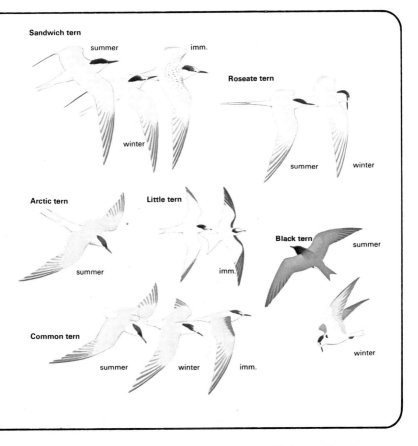

Sandwich tern

summer

imm.

Roseate tern

winter

summer

winter

Arctic tern

Little tern

summer

imm.

Black tern

summer

Common tern

winter

summer

winter

imm.

southern Sweden, north-western France and Mediterranean in isolated colonies.

Roseate tern *37 cm S*

Paler wings than either common or Arctic terns and long, more deeply forked tail. Nests on coasts, often with common and Arctic terns, in British Isles and north-western France.

Arctic tern *37 cm S*

Entirely red bill, white streak below eye and translucent

wing-tips, unlike common tern. Black legs in winter. Nests on seashores and coastal marshes in north-western Europe.

Common tern *35 cm S*

Easily confused with Arctic tern, but has lighter underparts, darker underside of wing-tips and a black tip on bill. Red legs in winter. Breeds on seashores and inland waters, such as gravel pits, across Europe. N.B. All these terns migrate south to Africa in winter.

Little tern *23 cm S*

Small with short tail, white forehead and yellow, black-tipped bill. Active, noisy and flies with fast-beating wings. Nests on sandy or shingle beaches on European coasts.

Black tern *24 cm P*

Immatures and winter adults darker than little terns. Breeds on marshes and lakes across Europe. Seen on coast outside breeding season.

Great black-backed gull

imm.

Lesser black-backed gull

2nd summer

imm.

Great black-backed gull
69 cm RSW

Very large with heavy bill. Wings seem blacker than lesser black-backed gull's. Wing-beats are slow. Immatures are bigger and have heavier-looking bills than immature lesser black-backed and herring gulls. Breeds on coasts of northern Europe, and winters round to southern France.

Lesser black-backed gull
53 cm RSWP

Difficult to distinguish from above, but smaller and slighter (and more common). Immatures very difficult to tell from immature herring gulls, except that in second winter their legs become yellow. Breeds on coasts of northern Europe, but seen inland in winter.

Herring gull *56 cm RW*

Similar size to lesser black-backed gull, but with silver grey back and wings. Immatures very similar to immature lesser black-backed gulls. Breeds on sea coasts, cliffs and houses throughout Europe. Seen inland feeding on rubbish dumps and ploughed fields, and roosts on playing fields and open spaces.

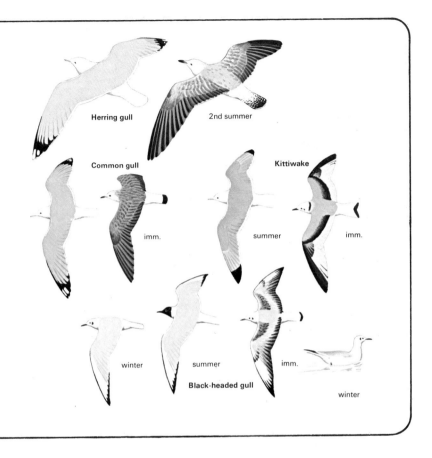

Herring gull

2nd summer

Common gull

Kittiwake

imm.

summer

imm.

winter

summer

imm.

Black-headed gull

winter

Common gull *41 cm RSWP*

Looks like a smaller, more slender herring gull, but has yellow-green legs and no red spot on bill. Wing shape is blunter than black-headed gull's. Breeds on coasts and inland waters in Ireland, Scotland, Netherlands, Germany and Scandinavia, with isolated colonies elsewhere.

Kittiwake *41 cm RS*

Daintiest gull. Similar to common gull but with no white on wing-tips, and with black legs. Immatures have black collars, distinctive black pattern on wings and black tip to tail. Breeds on sea cliffs of British Isles, north-western France, Norway and Iceland; rest of year spent at sea.

Black-headed gull *41 cm RSWP*

Adult in summer has chocolate-coloured head and scarlet legs. Outside breeding season it is white with brownish mark behind the head. Immatures have brown speckles on back and black band on end of tail. Breeds on marshes, upland bogs, coastal dunes and shingle in northern and central Europe. Often seen inland in winter.

Great skua

Arctic skua

light phase

imm.

dark phase

Manx shearwater

Fulmar

'blue' phase

Great skua *58 cm SP*

Same size as herring gull, but more thickset and with shorter wings and tail. Darker than immature gulls, with marked white wing flashes and more angled wings. Breeds in northern Scotland and winters in north Atlantic.

Arctic skua *46 cm SP*

More slender and smaller than great skua with narrower wings and longer tail. Dark and light colour phases. Breeds in far north of Scotland and Scandinavia.

Fulmar *47 cm RS*

Like a gull, but look carefully for the narrow, rather straight wings and 'tube-nose' of a petrel. Head seems rather large. Back and wings are silver grey. Breeds on cliffs all around British Isles (including some places inland), and Norway, having spread rapidly in recent years. Returns to breeding sites in November and December and leaves for oceans in August.

Manx shearwater *35 cm SP*

Long, very narrow wings and largish bill. Glides low over surface of sea, using air currents and flicking over to show pale underside and then dark back. Nests in burrows on islands on west coasts of British Isles and in southern Mediterranean. Breeding season: February to September. Usually at sea for rest of year.

Brent Goose *56–61 cm W*

About the size of mallard. Two races: dark-breasted form from Arctic Russia wintering on North Sea coasts and estuaries, and light-bellied form from Greenland, Spitsbergen and Canada, wintering in Ireland and parts of North Sea coasts. Found in flocks.

Eider *58 cm RW*

Males' eclipse plumage and immature males' plumage may confuse. Look for black under-parts. Flies low over sea in flocks (looser than scoters). Breeds in northern British Isles and Scandinavia. Winters north from Biscay.

Shelduck *61 cm RS*

Long legs and upright stance similar to geese. Males have knob on bill, otherwise similar to females. Immatures have no chestnut breast band. Breeds on coasts of British Isles, northern and eastern Europe.

Common scoter *48 cm RWP*

Female may be confused with smaller female long-tailed duck. Flies in tight flocks low over sea. Breeds in Northern Ireland, Scotland and Scandinavia. Winters on coasts of western Europe and north Africa.

Long-tailed duck ♂ *53 cm* ♀ *41 cm W*

Female larger than male; brown, with pale face and underparts. Winters on coasts of northern Europe.

Gannet *90 cm S*

Long, thin wings with black ends, torpedo-shaped body and grey bill. Pale orange-yellow head, and feet black with greenish lines (bluer in females and yellower in males). Immatures are dark brown, speckled with cream. Breeds in colonies in British Isles, Channel Islands, Iceland and Norway. Moves south-west into Atlantic in winter.

Shag *76 cm R*

Smaller and more uniformly dark than cormorant. Distinctive crest in breeding season. Usually flies low over water. When swimming, holds head at less of an angle than cormorant. Breeds on rocky coasts in northern Europe and Mediterranean.

Cormorant *90 cm RSW*

Unmistakable when hanging out wings to dry. Breeding adults can be told from shags by white face and white patch on thighs, and juveniles and immatures are darker and heavier-looking. Often flies high and can be told from

Great northern diver

winter

Black-throated diver

summer

Black-throated diver

winter

ducks and geese by the lengths of tail and bill. Breeds on coasts, nesting in rocks and cliffs, in Iceland, British Isles, Norway and north-western France and, in northern and southern Europe, in trees. May be seen inland in winter.

Great northern diver
68–80 cm W

Breeding plumage unmistakable. In winter plumage, larger, heavier-looking and with thicker, straighter bill than red-throated and black-throated divers. Found around northern European coasts in winter.

Black-throated diver
58–68 cm RWP

Black throat, grey head, black-and-white stripes on neck, black-and-white 'checked' back than red-throated diver. In winter has darker brown back than red-throated diver. Seen around coasts in winter, and breeds north of Scotland and Scandinavia.

summer

Red-throated diver

winter

Great crested grebe

summer

imms.

winter

winter

winter

Great crested grebe

Red-necked grebe

Black-necked grebe

Red-throated diver
53–58 cm RWP

Red patch on throat, grey head and neck, black-and-white striped neck, dark back. Swims low in water, which it leaves only to visit nest. Smaller, thinner-necked and more up-right than black-throated diver. Note up-tilted bill. Winters on inland waters and around coasts, and breeds on edges of moorland lakes in Northern Ireland, Scotland, Scandinavia and Iceland.

Great crested grebe *48 cm R*

Long neck, sharp pointed bill and feather-tufts around the face make it unmistakable. In flight has white patches on wing. Crest and thinner neck separate it from divers. Young are striped and when small are sometimes carried on backs of parents. Nests on gravel pits, reservoirs and meres from low-lands of Scotland south across Europe to Africa.

Red-necked grebe *43 cm W*

White face, red neck and yellow bill in breeding plumage. Black and yellow bill, dark grey neck and dark crown coming below eye separate it from great crested grebe in winter. In flight, leading edge of wing is less white. Breeds in eastern Europe, and winters on North Sea and English Channel coasts.

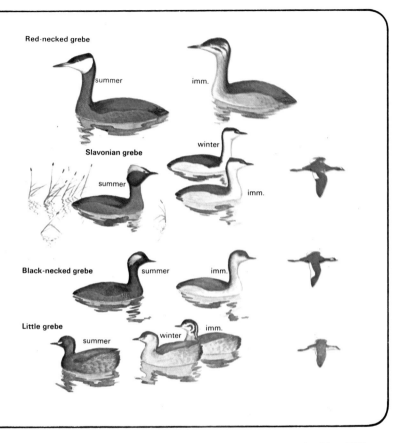

Red-necked grebe
summer
imm.

Slavonian grebe
winter
summer
imm.

Black-necked grebe
summer
imm.

Little grebe
winter
imm.
summer

Slavonian grebe *33 cm RWP*

Red neck, upward-pointing crests and yellow-tipped bill make this different from black-necked grebe. Breeds on lakes with plenty of vegetation around the edges in Scottish Highlands, Scandinavia and eastern Europe.

Black-necked grebe *30 cm RWP*

Has black neck and downward-pointed tufts. Breeds on pools with plenty of vegetation in isolated places in British Isles and central and southern Europe. In winter, hard to distinguish from Slavonian grebe. Bill of black-necked grebe is slightly turned up, and black cap comes below the eye, however. Slavonian grebes are more often found on coasts in winter and tend to appear singly, while black-necked grebes prefer inland waters and may be seen in flocks.

Little grebe *27 cm RWP*

Most widespread and numerous grebe. Small, with chestnut throat, and at base of bill a yellow patch (which disappears in winter). Breeds on lakes and rivers where there is luxuriant vegetation, throughout Europe, but not Scandinavia. Smaller and tubbier than moorhen (see page 132)

125

Mute swan

Whooper swan

imm.

imm.

Canada goose

Bewick's swan

imm.

Mute swan *152 cm R*

Distinguished from other swans by its orange bill with black basal knob (larger in male). Immatures are brown. Neck outstretched when flying. Hisses when angry. Breeds in north-western Europe.

Whooper swan *152 cm W*

Has yellow and black bill with no basal knob. Very long, thin neck, which it holds more upright than mute swan. Honking call. Breeds in Iceland

Spitsbergen and Russia, and winters in north-western Europe.

Canada goose *92–102 cm R*

Bigger than barnacle goose, and with white on throat. Breeds on lakes, ponds and marshland in British Isles and southern Sweden. Winters on inland water and occasionally in coastal areas.

Bewick's swan *122 cm W*

Smaller, shorter neck than

whooper swan, with less yellow on bill. Honking call, higher pitched than whooper swan. Breeds in Spitsbergen and Russia. Winters in England, Ireland and Netherlands.

Greylag goose *76–89 cm WR*

Large, with heavy flight and walk. Pale grey forewing and dark trailing edge of wing shows in flight. Orange bill and pink legs. Honks loudly in flight. Breeds in Iceland, Norway, Denmark, Netherlands,

Greylag goose

Pink-footed goose

Eurasian race

Greenland race

Barnacle goose

White-fronted goose

imm.

Germany and north-west Scotland. Escaped and released birds breed elsewhere. Winters in northern and eastern Europe.

Pink-footed goose *61–76 cm W*

Smaller and darker than greylag goose, with which it is often seen in flocks in winter. Has smaller, darker head with short orange-and-black bill. Noisy, with *wink-wink* call. Breeds in tundra and winters in British Isles, Belgium and Netherlands.

Barnacle goose *58–69 cm W*

Only goose with white face and black neck. Breeds in Arctic. Winters in northern Britain, Ireland, Scandinavia and Holland on estuaries, marshes and grassland within reach of sea. Widely kept in captivity, and birds seen in summer or inland are probably escapes.

White-fronted goose *66–76 cm W*

White forehead and heavily marked underparts separate white-fronted geese from other grey geese. Bill pink (Eurasian race) or orange (Greenland race). Bubbling call–has been compared with cries of small hounds. Breeds in Arctic Circle and Greenland.

Mallard

♂

♀

♀

♂

Gadwall

♂

♀

♀

♂

Wigeon

♂

♀

♀

♂

Mallard *58 cm RW*

Commonest duck. Male has green head, white collar, purple/brown breast. Female speckled crown. Both sexes have large blue specula which show on the wings, especially in flight. Male in eclipse plumage has yellow bill. Breeds throughout Europe near fresh water. Winters on inland waters and on coasts.

Gadwall *51 cm RSW*

Male mainly grey with chest-nut, black-and-white showing on wing. Female similar to mallard but with pale under-side. In flight white speculum shows. Breeds on lowland inland water and marshes in eastern Britain, Netherlands, Germany, Austria and southern France. Winters in most of Europe (not Scandinavia) and North America.

Wigeon *46 cm RW*

Female is smaller than female mallard. Green speculum in both sexes. Flies fast, often in flocks. Whistles. Often grazes in fields. Breeds northern Britain, Iceland and Scandinavia.

Pintail *♂ 66 cm ♀ 56 cm RW*

Female similar to female wigeon but larger and more slender with pointed tail. Male has green and white speculum, female is brown. In flight wings look narrower than mallard's and female shows light belly. Flies fast. Found on fresh water, salt marshes, moors

Pintail

Shoveler

Garganey

Teal

and tundra in Scotland, Iceland, Netherlands, Germany, Denmark and Scandinavia, and occasionally elsewhere in Europe. Winters on inland waters, coastal marshes and estuaries.

Shoveler *51 cm RW*

Heavy shovel-like bill. Both sexes have blue forewing and green speculum. Breeds on lowland marshes with plenty of vegetation, in British Isles, Iceland, southern Sweden,

France to Denmark and Germany. Winters on inland waters and sometimes seacoasts.

Garganey *38 cm S*

Female similar to female teal but with more distinct eye-stripe and pale grey forewing. Speculum green and white with no black. Breeds in low-lying marshy areas and well-vegetated water in England and across Europe (except in Spain and southern Italy). Winters southern Europe and Africa.

Teal *35 cm RW*

Female looks like very small mallard. Both have green and black specula. Flies very fast, often in flocks. Breeds all over Europe (except Spain, Italy and Balkans) in marshes, well-vegetated lakes and rivers. Winters on inland water, coasts and estuaries.

Red-crested pochard
56 cm R

Female brown with light face and throat, and pink-tipped bill. In flight both sexes show white wing bar. Feeds on marshes and reed-fringed lakes in East Anglia, Netherlands, France, Spain, Austria and Italy

Scaup *48 cm W*

Female has more white at base of bill than·tufted duck. Breeds near freshwater lakes in tundra. Winters mainly on coasts.

Pochard *46 cm RW*

Female has brown head, neck and breast; body grey. In flight both sexes show contrast between throat and underparts and neither have white wing-bars. Breeds near slow-flowing and still fresh water and brackish lakes, in British Isles westward to Russia. Winters in British Isles south through Europe.

Tufted duck *43 cm RW*

Note crest of male. Female has

small crest, is brown and sometimes has white at base of bill (see scaup). Looks small in flight, with short wings. Breeds in slow-moving or still water in northern and eastern Europe, and winters on inland water.

Ferruginous duck *43 cm*

Female darker than female pochard and with white undertail coverts. Both sexes show white wing bar in flight. Breeds in brackish, fresh, still or slow-moving water and reedmarsh in

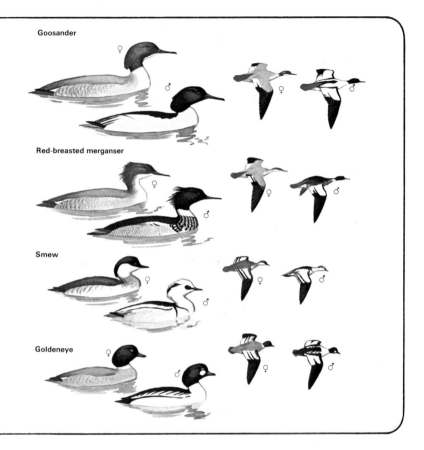

Goosander ♀ ♂

Red-breasted merganser ♀ ♂

Smew ♀ ♂

Goldeneye ♀ ♂

East Germany, parts of France, Italy, Spain and the Balkans.

Goosander *66 cm WR*

Male in breeding plumage has pale breast. Females, immatures and winter plumage males very similar to merganser but have less rigid crests. Note extent of brown on head. Breeds in holes in trees near lakes, rivers and fast streams. Found in Scotland, northern England, north Wales, Scandinavia, Iceland and Germany.

Red-breasted merganser *58 cm WR*

In breeding plumage male has brown breast. Outside breeding season male is similar to female and immatures. Note that russet on neck does not extend all round. Breeds in Iceland, Scandinavia, northern Germany and British Isles.

Smew *41 cm W*

Male in breeding plumage looks very white. Breeds on water in conifer forests in northern Scandinavia and Russia. Winters in southern England, Scandinavia to Mediterranean on fresh water and estuaries.

Goldeneye *46 cm WR*

Female and immatures have a brown head and grey back and body. Breeds in holes in trees in Scandinavia, parts of Germany, eastern Russia and, very rarely, in Scotland. Winters on inland lakes and coasts.

Moorhen *33 cm RW*

Note red bill, flicking white tail feathers, and dark plumage with white line along side. Immatures browner with brown-grey bill. Feeds near water's edge or in fields near water. Distinguished from coot when swimming by its jerking head, and up-turned tail. Breeds on fresh water with plenty of vegetation throughout Europe except northern Scandinavia.

Coot *38 cm RW*

Adult has white bill and forehead and a more slaty back than moorhen. When swimming, has 'humped' back. Often feeds by diving. Immature brown with light-coloured neck and throat. Breeds on fresh water with plenty of vegetation, throughout Europe except northern Scandinavia. Forms flocks in winter.

Water rail *28 cm RW*

Seen in the open more often in hard weather. Makes grunting, squealing noises. Long bill and legs. Breeds in marshes and reedbeds throughout Europe except northern Scandinavia.

imm.

Heron

imm.

Spoonbill

imm.

Bittern

Heron *90 cm RW*

Grey and white. Adult has black eyestripe and crest. Immature has grey neck. In flight has slow wing-beats, legs outstretched and neck tucked back. Breeds in western Europe in colonies, usually in trees. Feeds and winters on all types of water, including sea-coasts and estuaries.

Spoonbill *86 cm S*

Immature has blackish wing-tips and pale bill. Breeds in Netherlands and southern Europe, nesting colonially in trees and reedbeds. Feeds in shallow fresh water, saltwater lagoons and estuaries.

Bittern *76 cm R*

Brown with green legs. Often sits hunched up, but stretches up when alarmed. Breeds in reed marshes and rarely seen, but may be heard 'booming'. In flight it has slow wing-beats and deep chest, looking rather like an owl with legs out-stretched. Breeds in parts of England and most western European countries except Norway.

Bearded tit ♀

Reed bunting ♂

Reed bunting ♀

Bearded tit ♂

imm.

imm.

Kingfisher

Dipper

Grey wagtail ♀

♂

Bearded tit *14 cm RW*

Very acrobatic and nimble in reeds. Call high-pitched, like stones being clinked. Breeds in reedbeds in East Anglia, Netherlands, Baltic coast and southern Europe.

Reed bunting *15 cm RW*

Female may be confused with a sparrow, but note face pattern and white outer tail feathers. Breeds in reedbeds and banks with plenty of vegetation throughout Europe.

Kingfisher *16·5 cm R*

Penetrating *chee* call. Dives from perch and hovers to catch fish. Found on inland waters in summer, also estuaries and coasts in winter. Breeds in nest tunnel, south from lowland Scotland and southern Sweden.

Dipper *18 cm R*

Brown and white, rather like a large, dark brown and white wren. Bobbing movement when walking amongst boulders on fast-flowing

rivers. Always found near water. Breeds in suitable habitats throughout Europe.

Grey wagtail *18 cm R*

Male loses black throat in winter. Bounding flight. Breeds near fast-running water in British Isles, and Europe to eastern Germany and southern Sweden.

Great reed warbler *19 cm*

Almost starling sized. More noticeable eye-stripe than reed

Savi's warbler

Reed warbler

Great reed warbler

Grasshopper warbler

Cetti's warbler

Sedge warbler

warbler's. Loud 'frog-like' song. Breeds in reedbeds and other freshwater margins throughout Europe, except British Isles and Scandinavia.

Reed warbler *12·5 cm S*

Note elongated forehead and rounded tail. Song is a continual churring clink. Breeds in reedbeds across Europe.

Savi's warbler *14 cm S*

Larger than grasshopper warbler and unstreaked. Loud,

low-pitched, slower song. Breeds in marshes and fens across Europe. Very rare breeding bird in British Isles.

Grasshopper warbler *13 cm S*

Very striped with rounded tail. Skulking, and usually noticed by grasshopper-like song. Breeds in marshes, also scrub, heath and other open habitats, across Europe.

Cetti's warbler *14 cm S*

Loud, 'explosive' song. Breeds in dense vegetation near water, in southern Europe and, rarely, in British Isles.

Sedge warbler *13 cm S*

Note striped head, buff eye-stripe and square-ended tail. Song is contrasting harsh and sweet notes. Breeds in coarse vegetation, bushes and hedges near water, throughout Europe except Spain and southern France.

135

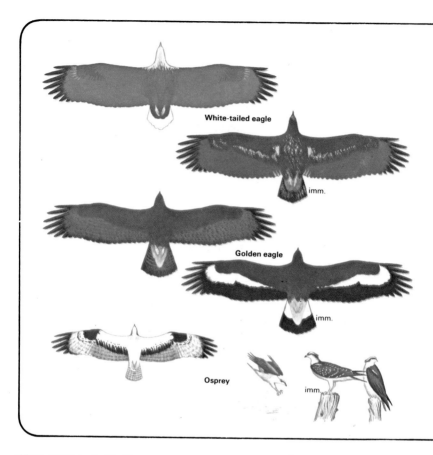

White-tailed eagle

imm.

Golden eagle

imm.

Osprey

imm.

White-tailed eagle *69–91 cm W*

Large and heavy-looking. Large prominent head. Edges of wings almost straight. Wings held flat or almost when soaring. Wedge-shaped tail is white in adult. Breeds on rocky coasts near water in large forests in Scandinavia and eastern Europe. Introduced to island of Rhum.

Golden eagle *75–88 cm R*

Large, but unless other birds are present for comparison it may seem smaller. Wings may seem curved. Tail very noticeable. Adult from below appears dark, but from above pale head and patches on wings may be seen. Immature has white tail band above and below; from below, white wing patches, and from above, smaller wing patches. Much larger than buzzard (see page 138). Breeds in mountains in Scotland, Scandinavia and Spain, and across to eastern Europe.

Osprey *51–58 cm S*

Long, noticeably angled wings (rather gull-like). Head small but protruding. Tail longish. Pale underside with barred wings. Breeds in trees, near water in Scotland, southern Spain, Scandinavia and eastwards.

Griffon vulture *97–104 cm*

Very large and pale. In flight wings seem more curved than black vulture's. Contrast shows between pale forewings and

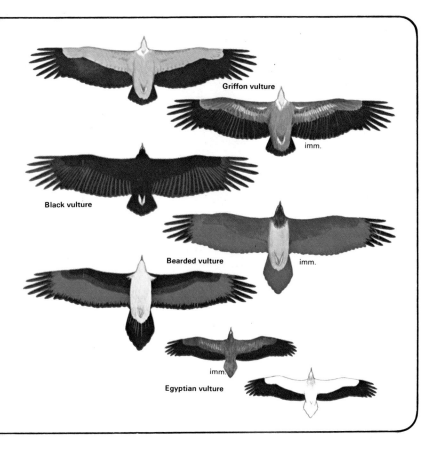

Griffon vulture

imm.

Black vulture

Bearded vulture

imm.

imm.

Egyptian vulture

black trailing edge. Feet not visible in flight. Pale neck ruff can be seen. Breeds in mountainous, rocky country in Spain, Sardinia, Sicily and eastern Mediterranean.

Black vulture *99–107 cm*

Very large with broad, straight wings and small head. Darker than griffon vulture. Wings held flat when soaring, not in shallow V-shape like griffon vulture. Pale feet sometimes show. Breeds in open country

in Spain, Majorca, Sardinia, Sicily and Balkans.

Bearded vulture *102–114 cm*

Large with pointed, angled wings, diamond-shaped tail and small, but protruding head. Adult has creamy underparts, and black wings and tail. Juvenile dark brown. Breeds in mountains in Pyrenees, Spain, Corsica, Sardinia and Balkans.

Egyptian vulture *58–66 cm*

Small, black and white, with

longer bill than other vultures. More lightly built than others. Tail wedge-shaped. Black and white flight pattern much more contrasting than griffon vulture's. Flight pattern is similar to white stork's. Immatures dark. Breeds in open country around Mediterranean.

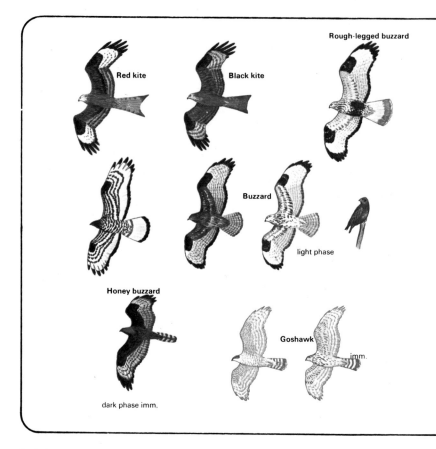

Rough-legged buzzard

Red kite

Black kite

Buzzard

light phase

Honey buzzard

Goshawk

imm.

dark phase imm.

Red kite *61 cm R*

Long, angled wings. Forked tail. Breeds in deciduous woodland in Wales and southwards from Germany and France.

Black kite *56 cm*

Long, angled wings. Tail with slight fork. No white on wings. Glides with wings level. Often breeds near towns, villages and water, in most of Europe except British Isles, Scandinavia, Belgium and Netherlands. Migrates south in winter.

Rough-legged buzzard *51–61 cm W*

Black patch on wing. Breeds in open country in northern Scandinavia, and winters south-eastwards across Europe.

Honey buzzard *51–58 cm S*

Wings narrower at base than buzzard's and barred. Breeds in forests across Europe from southern England and Sweden.

Buzzard *51–56 cm R*

Variable colours. Breeds

in forests and woods, across Europe (not Ireland).

Goshawk *48–51 cm R*

Rounded wings. Finely barred body and underwings, and long, barred tail. Flight is a series of quick wing-beats followed by short glides. Breeds in forests across Europe.

Bonelli's eagle *66–74 cm*

Parallel wing-edges. Small but protruding head. Soars and glides with vigorous beats

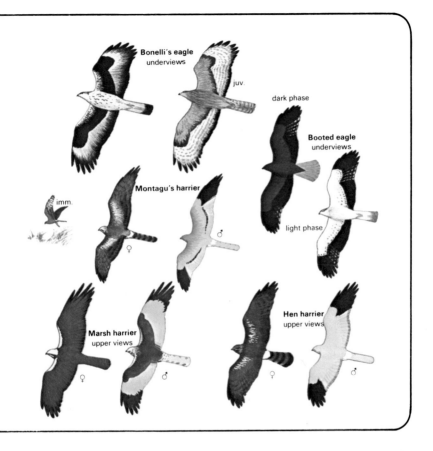

Bonelli's eagle
underviews

juv.

dark phase

Booted eagle
underviews

imm.

Montagu's harrier

♂

light phase

♀

Hen harrier
upper views

Marsh harrier
upper views

♀

♂

♀

♂

when flying. Breeds on wooded mountains in southern Europe. Winters in open country.

Montagu's harrier
41–46 cm S

Immature has unstreaked, rufous underparts. Breeds on farmland, grassland and edges of wetland from England across Europe. Winters in Africa.

Booted eagle *46–53 cm*

Two colour phases—light has

pale underparts contrasting with black on wings. Dark phase could be confused with marsh harrier and black kite but it soars on flat wings, and has square-ended tail. Breeds on wooded hills in Spain, France and eastern Europe. Winters in more open country in Africa.

Marsh harrier *48–56 cm SR*

Adult male usually has grey on wings. Females and immatures darker, with cream on head and

leading edge of wings. Breeds in Europe from eastern England to southern Sweden, and southwards. Winters in southern Europe and North Africa.

Hen harrier *43–51 cm RW*

Wings held in V-shape when soaring. Male grey with white underparts. Female and immature difficult to distinguish from female Montagu's harrier, although larger. Breeds on moorland, marshes and reedbeds across Europe.

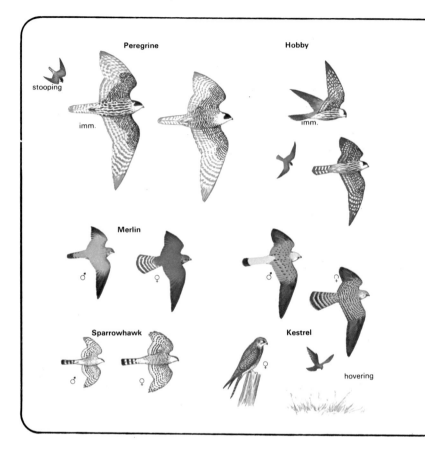

Peregrine *38–48 cm RW*

Pointed, curved wings and shortish tail. Bluish-grey upperparts with barred underparts. Immature brown with streaked breast and barred underwings. Flies strongly but with rather shallow wing-beats, glides and swoops very fast at flying birds. Breeds in upland areas and cliffs across Europe. Winters on marshes and coasts.

Hobby *30–36 cm S*

Long-winged, with longish tail. In flight looks like a large swift. White cheeks contrast with dark moustache. Russet thighs and undertail show in adult in flight. Breeds in open country with trees across Europe from southern England. Winters in Africa.

Merlin *27–33 cm RSW*

Small, compact falcon. Shortish square tail. Flies straight, with fast wing-beats and short glides. Breeds on hills and moors in northern Europe.

Winters in southern Europe.

Kestrel *34 cm RSW*

Hovers when hunting. Long, pointed wings and long tail. Male has grey head and tail with brown, black-flecked back. Female is brown with barred back and tail. Nests in open country across Europe. Often seen hunting over roadside verges.

Sparrowhawk *28–38 cm RW*

Long tail and short, broad

Eagle owl

Snowy owl

pale subspecies

Barn owl

Long-eared owl

Short-eared owl

dark subspecies

wings. Fast flier, dashing
through trees or along hedges
after small birds. Breeds in
wooded areas across Europe.
In British Isles more common
in west and north.

Eagle owl *56 cm*

Large, brown, 'eared' owl with
large orange eyes. Hunts at
dawn and dusk, as well as
during night. Breeds Scandinavia, Germany, south-east
France, Spain, Austria, Switzerland, Italy and eastwards.

Snowy owl *53–66 cm RW*

Large and mainly white, with
brown bars on female. Hunts in
daylight. Breeds high moorland
and tundra in Iceland, Scandinavia and Shetland. May be
seen on coasts in winter.

Barn owl *34 cm R*

Long wings. Screeching call.
Hunts at night. Breeds on
farmland and in open country,
usually in buildings and ruins,
across Europe, but not Norway
and Sweden.

Long-eared owl *36 cm RW*

Long 'ear' tufts. Face has pale
markings. Long, slow wing-
beats. Call a long, drawn-out
hoot. Breeds in conifers across
Europe except northern Scandinavia. Winters in open country

Short-eared owl *38 cm RW*

Black wing-tips. Hunts by day.
Barking flight-call. Breeds in
open country across northern
Europe. Some winter south into
north Africa.

141

Tawny owl

rufous phase   grey phase

Tengmalm's owl

Little owl

imm.

Scops owl

Pygmy owl

Tawny owl *38 cm R*

Round-looking brown or grey owl. Short, broad wings. Hunts at night. Calls are hoots and squeaks. Breeds in open woodland, parks and large gardens across Europe, except Ireland and northern Scandinavia.

Tengmalm's owl *25 cm*

Square head with white face. Adult shows white on back in flight. Mellow rising, then falling, hoot. Breeds in conifer forests in Scandinavia. Ger-

many, Austria and Switzerland.

Little owl *22 cm R*

Light face, well-marked head and breast. Very short tail. Often perches. Bounding flight. Breeds in farmland and open country south from lowlands of Scotland across Europe, but not in Ireland, Norway or Sweden.

Pygmy owl *16·5 cm*

Very small and dumpy with noticeable tail. Piping hoot.

Hunts day or night. Breeds in coniferous forests in upland areas in Scandinavia, Germany, Austria and Switzerland.

Scops owl *19 cm*

Very small, with 'ear' tufts. Upright stance. Hunts at night. Bell-like call. Breeds in southern Europe in open woodland, farmland and outskirts of towns.

Pheasant *53–89 cm R*

Plumage of male varies, but

Pheasant

♂ ♀ ♂

Partridge

♂ ♀ imm.

flight rear view

Red-legged partridge

imm.

Corncrake   Quail   ♀

♂

flight rear view

head always green with red
wattle. Immatures long-legged
and skinny. Noisy guttural call.
Breeds in open country with
woods, sometimes in reedbeds,
throughout Europe except
extreme south and north.

Partridge *30 cm R*

Smaller and rounder than
pheasant. Brown horseshoe
mark on breast of males and
some females. Runs fast, does
not perch above ground. High-
pitched call. Breeds in open

country, usually lowland,
across most of Europe.

Red-legged partridge
34 cm R

Black band and spotting on
upper breast. Note bars on
flanks and white face. Call
sounds like 'chuka-chuka'.
Breeds in open country in
England and south-eastern
Europe.

Corncrake *27 cm S*

Member of rail family. Russet

patches on wings and dangling
legs in flight separate it from
young partridges and quail.
Call similar to comb being
flicked – 'crex-crex'. More often
seen than heard. Breeds in
rough grassland and hayfields
from Ireland across Europe.

Quail *18 cm S*

Rarely seen but high-pitched
'wet-my-lips' call is unmistakeable. Breeds on farmland in
southern British Isles, across
Europe except Scandinavia.

Capercaillie ♂ 86 cm ♀ 62 cm R

Very big and turkey-like. Female could be mistaken for much smaller female black grouse but has orange patch on breast. Male sounds like man laughing gently, female like pheasant. Breeds in conifer forests in northern Spain, Scottish Highlands, Scandinavia and central Europe.

Black grouse ♂ 53 cm ♀ 41 cm

Male black and white with lyre-shaped tail. Female much smaller, grey-brown and with forked tail. Breeds on margins of moorland, woodland and upland in Britain, Scandinavia, Germany, Austria, Switzerland.

Hazel hen 35–36 cm

Black band on tail shows in flight. Male has black throat. Breeds in mixed woodland from Russia to Scandinavia.

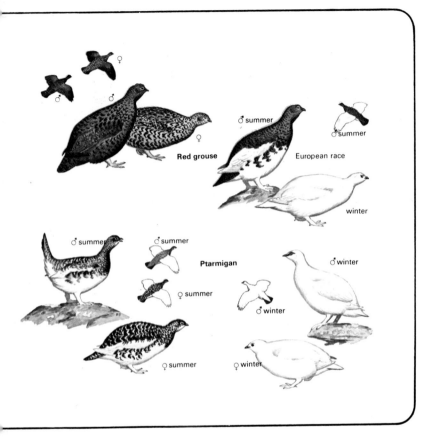

Red grouse

European race

winter

♂ summer

♂ summer

Ptarmigan

♂ winter

♀ summer

♂ winter

♀ summer

♀ winter

Red grouse/willow grouse
38–41 cm R

Scottish variety is dark with white legs (red grouse). In Scandinavia has white breast and wings (willow grouse), and becomes white in winter. Found at lower levels than very similar ptarmigan. Breeds on heath, moorland and tundra, sometimes coming down to farmland in winter.

Ptarmigan *32–36 cm R*

Totally white in winter except for black tail. Can be distinguished from willow grouse by smaller body, slender bill and more feathered feet, male with black between lores (the space between the eye and bill). In summer male becomes dark grey-brown with white belly and wings, and female is barred golden brown. In autumn male has grey back and white underparts. Breeds on mountain tops and tundra in Scottish Highlands, Pyrenees, Scandinavia and Iceland.

Oystercatcher

summer

imm.

winter

Avocet

imm.

Lapwing

Turnstone

summer

winter

summer

imm.

Oystercatcher *43 cm RSW*

Note winter plumage. Juvenile has paler legs and bill with dark tip. Wing-bars show in flight. Shrill, rapid piping call. Breeds on seacoasts and river valleys in uplands in north-western Europe. Winters on coasts around Europe.

Avocet *43 cm RSW*

Black and white with up-turned bill. Blue legs. Wades in water and swims. Klinking call. Breeds on salt marshes and fresh water marshes in East Anglia, Netherlands, Denmark, southern Spain and eastern Europe. Found in winter on estuaries.

Lapwing *30 cm RSW*

Long crest, shorter in im-mature. Short bill. Rounded, black wing-tips show in flight. Call is high-pitched 'pee-wit'. Found in flocks except during breeding season. Breeds in almost all types of open country including farmland, moorland and marshes through-out northern Europe. Winters in open country, coasts and estuaries in north-western and southern Europe.

Turnstone *23 cm W*

Black throat and tortoiseshell back in summer. Grey back and smudged black throat in winter. Short-legged. Breeds on tundra and coasts in Scandinavia. Winters on seacoasts, especially with rocks.

Grey plover *28 cm W*

Plumper and greyer than golden plover. Shows black patches under wings near body in flight. Looser flocks than golden plover. Breeds on Russian tundra. Winters on coasts of British Isles, western Europe and north Africa.

Ringed plover *19 cm RW*

White wing-bar in flight. Breeds on sandy or shingly seashores, also gravel pits in northern Europe. Winters on muddy shores and estuaries.

Golden plover *28 cm RW*

In summer black face, breast and underparts fringed with white with golden brown upperparts. In winter black areas become pale. Liquid call. Seen in flocks, often with lapwings. Note pointed wings. Breeds on moorland in Iceland, British Isles and Scandinavia. Winters on seashore, farmland and estuaries in Europe and Africa.

Little ringed plover *15 cm S*

Note pale legs, dark bill, yellow eye-ring and no white wing-bar. Breeds on sand and shingle beaches by fresh water across Europe (not Ireland).

Dotterel *22 cm S*

Chestnut breast, grey throat, eye-stripes that meet at back of neck. Paler in winter. Breeds in mountains, tundra and (in Netherlands) farmland. Found in Scotland, Scandinavia and eastern Europe.

winter

Knot

winter

winter

summer

summer

Sanderling

winter

winter

winter

Purple sandpiper   summer

summer

winter

autumn

summer

Dunlin   winter

autumn

Curlew sandpiper

Knot 25 cm W

Reddish summer plumage, grey
in winter. Breeds within Arctic
Circle and winters on estuaries
and muddy shores of western
Europe.

Sanderling 20 cm W

Black legs and bill. Runs jerkily
along tide edge. White wing-
bar in flight. Call – 'twick-twick'.
Breeds within Arctic Circle and
winters on coasts of western
Europe.

Purple sandpiper 21 cm W

Hunched, dumpy appearance.
Breeds in Iceland and northern
Scandinavia and winters on
rocky coasts of northern Europe.

Dunlin 17–19 cm RSW

Slightly down-curved bill. Thin
white wing-bars and white
sides to rump show in flight.
Call – high-pitched 'tweep'.
Breeds on moorland and bogs
n British Isles, Iceland,
Scandinavia and Baltic coast.
Winters on European coasts.

Curlew sandpiper 19 cm P

Noticeable eye-stripe. In flight
white rump shows (compare
sandpipers) and call is
'chirrup'. Breeds Arctic,
migrates to Africa in autumn.

Spotted redshank 30 cm PW

Longer legs and bill than
redshank. Immature plumage
like speckly redshank, without
white flash on wing. Call note–
clear 'too-it'. Breeds in
northern Scandinavia and
Russia. Winters in western

Spotted redshank

winter

winter

summer

Redshank

Green sandpiper

upper view

Little stint

autumn

summer

under view

imm.

Wood sandpiper

under view

upper view

Common sandpiper

Europe and Mediterranean.

Redshank *28 cm RPW*

White rump and white trailing
edges to wings in flight. Call –
three-note 'tew-hee-hee'.
Breeds in grassy meadows
near water, bogs and marshes
throughout Europe (not
central France and Germany).
Winters on coasts.

Green sandpiper *23 cm P*

Shorter-necked and smaller
than greenshank. 'Weet-weet'

call note. Breeds in swampy
woodlands in north-eastern
Europe. Winters in western and
southern Europe.

Little stint *13 cm PW*

Smallest European wader. Legs
black. Flight note 'chick'. Small
amount of white on rump.
Breeds in Russia, winters in
southern Europe and Africa.

Wood sandpiper *20·5 cm SP*

Longer legs and bill than common sandpiper. Note eye-stripes.

yellow legs protruding beyond
tail in flight and white rump.
Flat, triple call – 'twee-twee-
twee'. Breeds in northern
Europe. Winters in Africa.

Common sandpiper
19·5 cm PW

Tail has bobbing action. Broad
white wing-bars and dark tail
in flight. Flies low over water.
Breeds on upland rivers,
streams and estuaries through
most of Europe. Winters on
coasts of Europe and Africa.

Black-tailed godwit

winter

summer

Greenshank

winter

Ruff

♂ winter

Bar-tailed godwit

summer

♂ summer

Black-tailed godwit
41 cm SPW

Slightly larger and longer-legged than bar-tailed godwit. Less curved bill. Greyer in winter. Black and white tail and white wing-bars show in flight in winter and summer. Legs protrude in flight. Breeds in wet grassland in Iceland, East Anglia, Netherlands, Denmark and Germany.

Greenshank *30·5 cm SPW*

Large wedge of white on tail and back. Calls when flushed— 'chu-chu-chu'. Breeds in bogs, marshes and damp woodland clearings in Scottish Highlands and Scandinavia. Winters on marshes and estuaries in Europe and Mediterranean.

Bar-tailed godwit *38 cm PW*

Tail barred. In winter eye-stripe more prominent than black-tailed godwit's. In flight legs hardly show beyond end of tail, but note white wedge on back. Breeds in northern

Scandinavia and Russia. Winters on coasts of western Europe.

Ruff *♂ 29 cm ♀ 23 cm SPW*

Note small head and upright stance. Leg colour is *not* a reliable guide. Female smaller. Breeds in wet grassland and marshes in eastern England, Netherlands, south-western France, Scandinavia and northern Germany. Winters in shallow fresh and salt water in western Europe.

Curlew *53–58 cm RSPW*

Legs show beyond tail in flight. White rump. Call—'curwee, curwee'. Breeds on moorland and bogs in uplands of north-western Europe. Winters in wetlands and estuaries.

Whimbrel *41 cm SPW*

Twittering call. Breeds in Iceland, Shetland and northern Scandinavia. Winters in southern Europe, passing along European coasts.

Snipe *27 cm RW*

Note head pattern and bars on back. When flushed, flies with twisting flight. In flight russet-orange tail and pale trailing edge may show. Breeds in marsh, wet grazing land and bogs across Europe. Some winter in Mediterranean.

Woodcock *34 cm RW*

Long bill. Dumpy body. Flies with rather slow wing-beats with bill held pointing down-wards. Breeds in woods and heathland with trees, across Europe except most of Spain, Italy and the Balkans.

Jack snipe *19 cm PW*

Smaller and dumpier than snipe with comparatively shorter bill. Note head mark-ings. In flight wings appear stubby and stripes on back extend to tail. Rises abruptly when flushed. Breeds in northern Scandinavia and Russia. Winters on wetland in western and southern Europe.

Shorelark 16·5 cm W

Note dark tail with white tail feathers. Breeds on rocky ground and mountains in Scandinavia and Russia. Winters on east coasts of Britain and North Sea coast from north-eastern France to Baltic.

Lapland Bunting 15 cm PW

Male in winter shows blackish throat. Breeds on tundra in northern Scandinavia. Winters on east coasts of Britain, north-eastern France, Belgium, Netherlands and Denmark.

Snow bunting 16·5 cm RPW

Enormous variation in plumage during moult. Breeds in mountains, tundra and rocky coasts – Greenland, Iceland, Scottish Highlands and Scandinavia. Winters in northern European seashores.

Red-necked phalarope 18 cm SP

Small, often rather tame.
Swims. Female more brightly marked than male. Breeds in Iceland, north-western isles of Scotland, Shetland and Scandinavia. Winters at sea.

Grey Phalarope 20·5 cm PW

Red throat and underparts with white face in summer. Grey in winter with more uniformly grey back than red-necked phalarope and has shorter bill. Breeds in Iceland, Greenland and North America. Winters at sea.

Swift

Swallow

House martin

Sand martin

Swift *16·5 cm S*

Crescent-shaped wings. Short forked tail. Note different wing-shape from swallows and martins. Very dark brown except for light throat. Screaming call. Often flies in flocks. Nests in roofs and towers. Feeds over water, fields and buildings, often flying very high. Breeds in most of Europe, and winters in Africa.

Swallow *19 cm S*

Curved, dark blue wings and long tail streamers. Throat red in adult, cream in juvenile. Creamy underparts. Breeds in mud nests on buildings, over most of Europe. Feeds on insects swooping low over fields and water. Winters in South Africa.

House martin *12·5 cm S*

Dark blue back, with white rump and blue forked tail. Underside white. Broader wings than sand martin or swallow. Breeds in mud nests under eaves, over most of Europe. Feeds above buildings and fields, often along edges of woods. Winters in Africa.

Sand martin *12 cm S*

Small, with dark brown back and shallow-notched tail. Underside cream with brown band across breast. Breeds in colonies in sand-cliffs, quarries and steep river-banks, usually near water, over most of Europe. Usually feeds over water. Winters in Africa.

153

Skylark

Crested lark

Woodlark

Short-toed lark

Skylark *18 cm RPW*

White outer tail feathers and trailing edge to wings. Small crest—not present on juvenile. Flies high and sings above territory. Breeds in open country across Europe. Flocks feed in fields in winter. Never perches in trees.

Crested lark *17 cm*

Long crest. Buff outer tail feathers. Broad wings and short tail in flight. Breeds in open country across Europe from southern Scandinavia (not British Isles).

Woodlark *15 cm R*

Note short tail, small white patches on tail and black-and-white wing patches. Small crest. Nests on ground but perches in trees. Breeds in woodland edges, heath and parkland with scattered trees, across Europe except northern Britain and northern Scandinavia. Now very rare in England.

Short-toed lark *14 cm*

Pale breast and underparts with *no* streaks. Dark patches on sides of breast not easy to see in the field. Dark tail shows in flight. Breeds in dry, sandy, open country in southern Europe. Winters in Africa.

Pied wagtail *18 cm R*

Black and white. Female greyer. Mainland European form has grey back. Flight note—'chisick'. Breeds in open

Pied wagtail

♂

♀

juv.

♂ continental race

♂ blue-headed race

♂ Spanish race

Yellow wagtail

♂ British race

juv.

♀

Tree pipit

song flights

Tawny pipit

Meadow pipit

country including parks and gardens across Europe.

Yellow wagtail *16·5 cm S*

British race has yellow head. Other races have grey, blue and ashy heads. Breeds in damp grassland, usually near water. Winters in Africa.

Tree pipit *15 cm SP*

Small, brown-backed, with streaked breast. Can only be identified in the field by its spiralling song flight, which starts from perch in a tree and ends with bird dropping back to the perch with wings outspread. Breeds through Europe. Winters in Africa.

Meadow pipit *14·5 cm SRPW*

Song flight rising and falling, not spiralling. Jerky flight. Breeds in open countryside throughout Europe. Winters in open country in flocks.

Tawny pipit *16·5 cm*

Pale with streaks only on head. Juvenile has streaked breast. Longish, dark tail. Bounding flight. Breeds in dry, sandy country across Europe.

Roller

part of breeding colony

display flight

imm.

Bee-eater

Hoopoe

imm.

dusk silhouettes

♂

♀

Nightjar

Roller *31 cm*

Looks like brightly coloured crow. Bright blue wing-patches. even more noticeable than jay (see page 168). Direct flight. Harsh call. Breeds in open country in southern and eastern Europe. Winters in Africa.

Bee-eater *28 cm*

Brightly coloured, pointed wings, long central tail feathers (absent in juveniles). Down-curved bill. Breeds in open country, nesting colonially in tunnels in steep banks through Mediterranean Europe. Winters in Africa.

Hoopoe *28 cm P*

Unmistakable at rest or in flight. Black wings barred with white. Pinkish head, shoulders and underparts, barred wings and back and crest. Call is 'hoo-hoo-hoo'. Breeds in lowland farmland, parks and gardens in Europe (except Scandinavia and, usually, British Isles). Often feeds on rubbish dumps. Winters in Africa.

Nightjar *27 cm S*

Mottled brown and grey plumage makes nightjar very well camouflaged and almost impossible to find during the day. Flies with buoyant flight at dusk and night. Breeds in open woodland, heathland and open country with scattered trees throughout Europe, except northern Scandinavia.

northern race

southern race

Great grey shrike

Lesser grey shrike

imm.

♂ ♀

Woodchat shrike

Red-backed shrike

♂

♀

imm.

♂

Great grey shrike *24 cm W*

Long black tail with white outer feathers. Black wings with white bars and white strips on edges of grey back. Black eye-stripe. Often sits upright on bare branch. Dipping flight. Breeds in most of Europe (not British Isles). Winters in British Isles.

Lesser grey shrike *20 cm*

Note black forehead, stubbier bill, longer wings and shorter tail than great grey shrike.

Breeds in southern and eastern Europe.

Red-backed shrike *17 cm S*

Note grey head, grey rump, black-and-white tail and pinkish breast of male. Female has barred breast and brown back with no white. Perches or bushes. Breeds in most of Europe including southern England.

Woodchat shrike *17 cm A*

Note chestnut head and white

V-shape on back. Female dull grey-brown. Juveniles creamy brown. Often perches on telegraph wires. Breeds in southern and western Europe (not British Isles).

Icterine warbler — summer

Melodious warbler — summer, imm.

Willow warbler — imm.

Wood warbler

Bonelli's warbler

Chiffchaff

Icterine warbler *13·5 cm P*

Similar shape to reed warbler (see page 135). Note pale panel on sharply pointed wings. Breeds in Europe east from France (not Italy or Balkans) in open country – parks, gardens, woodland edges.

Melodious warbler *13 cm*

Similar to icterine warbler, but with shorter wings lacking pale area. Some adults and immatures quite pale. Breeds in France, Spain, Portugal and Italy. Habitat as for icterine warbler.

Willow warbler *11 cm S*

Very difficult to tell from chiffchaff. Usually has paler legs and more green plumage. Song is a series of descending notes. Found in woodland with trees and bushes, and gardens. Breeds in northern Europe from Pyrenees and Alps to northern Scandinavia.

Wood warbler *12·5 cm S*

Yellow throat, white belly, green back. Found in woods, especially beech, in most of Europe, north from Pyrenees, but not Ireland or northern Scandinavia.

Chiffchaff *11 cm S*

Greyer than willow warbler. Usually has dark legs. Monotonous 'zip-zap' song. Similar habitat to willow warbler. Breeds from southern Europe to southern Scandinavia.

Whitethroat ♀

song flight

Blackcap ♂

♂

♀

Lesser whitethroat

Dartford warbler ♂

Garden warbler

imm.

Bonelli's warbler *11·5 cm*

Yellowish patches on wings and rump. Found in woods on hillsides and mountains in southern Europe.

Whitethroat *14 cm S*

Note high crown, rufous in wings, and white throat of both male and female. Male's song flight conspicuous—bursts into song, flies up and plunges back into cover (scrub and hedgerows). Breeds across Europe.

Blackcap *14 cm SW*

Crown conspicuous—brown in female, black in male. Longer tail than garden warbler. Sings from cover. (Compare marsh tit and willow tit, page 177.) Breeds in most of Europe. Some stay during winter. Found in woods, scrub with trees and large gardens.

Lesser Whitethroat *13·5 cm S*

Note dark cheeks. Greyer above than whitethroat. Breeds in western Europe (not Italy or Spain) in scrub, open woods, parkland and gardens.

Garden warbler *14 cm S*

Roundish head and short bill. Breeds in most of Europe in woodland with plentiful undergrowth, parks and large gardens.

Dartford warbler *12·5 cm R*

Long tail. High forehead. Often sings from tops of bushes. Breeds in southern England and southern Europe.

159

Mistle thrush *27 cm RS*

Larger and greyer than other thrushes. White outer tail feathers. Heavy-looking with white underwing showing in flight. Long, undulating flight, with wings closing regularly. Loud song, delivered from treetops. Often first bird to sing after thunderstorms. Harsh call in flight. Breeds across Europe except Norway.

Song thrush *23 cm RPW*

Speckled underparts. No white on tail (see mistle thrush). No eye-stripe. Note underwing pattern in flight (see redwing). Clear song delivered from prominent perch. Shorter tail than blackbird. Breeds in woods, open country and gardens from northern Spain and Italy northwards.

Blackbird *25 cm RPW*

Yellow bill and yellow eye-ring in male. Darkness of females and juveniles varies. Screaming call. Jerky flight. Note habit of raising tail on landing. Male sings from prominent perch. Breeds in woods, forests and open areas with trees, through all Europe (except northern Scandinavia).

Fieldfare

juv.

Redwing

juv.

Ring ouzel

♂

♀

juv.

Fieldfare *25·5 cm RPW*

Grey head and rump, deep brown back, apricot breast and black tail. White underwing contrasted with grey wings. Call note is a harsh 'chack-chack'. Breeds in open woodland, parks and gardens in north-eastern Europe. Winters in most of Europe, usually seen in flocks, often with redwings, on berry-bearing bushes or fields.

Redwing *21 cm RPW*

Smaller and with more blurred speckling than song thrush. Note eye-stripe and red underwing. Flies in flocks with noticeable 'tseep' call. Difficult to tell from song thrush in flight but is slightly dumpier. Breeds in forests and open areas with scattered trees in Scandinavia, Iceland and far north of Scotland. Winters in western Europe.

Ring ouzel *24 cm SP*

Like blackbird with white crescent on throat. Female brown with crescent. Note absence of yellow eye-ring (see blackbird). Breeds in mountains and high moorland, north from Pyrenees.

Stonechat *12·5 cm RS*

Female lacks black head.
Male head becomes brown
in winter. Note dark tail in
flight. Breeds on moors,
heaths and bushy sea-cliffs in
western and southern Europe.

Whinchat *12·5 cm SP*

Note eye-stripe and wing
pattern on male and tail pattern
of female. Breeds in similar
habitat to stonechat; in Europe
from Scandinavia to northern
Spain and Italy.

Wheatear *14·5 cm SP*

Note white and black
tail. Breeds on uplands, downs
and open country across
Europe

Rock thrush *19 cm*

Reddish tail and white rump
make male unmistakeable.
Breeds on rocky mountains
in southern Europe.

Blue rock thrush *20 cm*

Female darker than rock thrush.
Breeds in rocky places in
southern Europe

Corn bunting

Yellowhammer

♀ ♂

Rock bunting

imm.

Cirl bunting

♀ ♂

♂

Ortolan bunting

♀ ♂

imm.

Corn bunting *18 cm R*

No white on tail or trailing edge of wings (see skylark). Breeds on farmland, dry hills and scrub across Europe (absent from Norway and most of Sweden).

Yellowhammer *16·5 cm R*

Females and juveniles less yellow. Call is an unmistakable, high-pitched, wheezy 'little-piece-of-bread-and-no-cheese'. Found in hedgerows, and scrub across Europe.

Rock bunting *16 cm*

Bold grey and black head and pale rufous underparts. Breeds on stony hillsides, gardens and vineyards in southern Europe.

Cirl bunting *16·5 cm R*

Females and juveniles less well marked. Compare with yellow-hammer. Breeds on farmland and hedges in western Europe from south-west England to Mediterranean and Balkans.

Ortolan bunting *16·5 cm P*

Females and juveniles duller. Breeds on cultivated land across Europe (not British Isles).

House sparrow

♂ summer

♂ winter

Linnet

♀

♂

Twite

Tree sparrow

♂ summer

♀ winter

Redpoll

imm

Goldfinch

♀ winter

House sparrow *14·5 cm R*

Slate-grey crown and large black throat patch of male unmistakable. Female grey-brown with eye-stripe and streaked back. Noisy. Wide-spread through Europe.

Tree sparrow *14 cm R*

Browner and more distinctly marked than house sparrow. Grey collar, black cheek patch and brown head distinguish it from male house sparrow. Sexes alike. Breeds in wood-land, parks and gardens across Europe.

Linnet *13·5 cm RS*

White on wings and tail can be seen in flight. Female duller. Breeds in open country from coast to mountains across Europe.

Twite *13·5 cm RSW*

Like female linnet, but note yellow bill and faint wing-bars in both sexes and pinkish rump in male. Breeds on open rocky moorland ground, usually high, but at sea level in western Ireland and Hebrides, Scotland. Norway. Winters on eastern coasts of Britain and North Sea and Baltic coasts.

Redpoll *14 cm RSPW*

Daintier than linnet. Note black chin. Shade of colouring varies through Europe. Breeds in most of Europe (except Spain and parts of France).

164

Chaffinch

♂

♀

♂

Brambling

♂ summer

Greenfinch

♀

♂ winter

♀

imm.

Bullfinch

♂

imm.

♀

Goldfinch *12 cm RS*

Call tinkling. Often feeds on thistles and teasels. Breeds in open country, gardens and orchards across Europe (except northern Scandinavia).

Chaffinch *15 cm RW*

White outer tail feathers, double wing-bars and olive rump distinctive in both sexes. Sings loudly from prominent perch. Breeds in woods, open areas with trees, parks and gardens across Europe.

Greenfinch *14·5 cm R*

Bright yellow wing-patches and yellow on tail in males, females and juveniles. Juveniles are streaked on both back and breast. Note heavy bill. Breeds in all Europe (except Scandinavia) in woodland edges, open country, parks and gardens.

Brambling *14·5 cm WP*

White rump and orange shoulders are distinctive. Note wing-bars in male in flight. Breeds in birch woods

and willow scrub in Scandinavia. Winters over the rest of Europe in open country.

Bullfinch *15 cm R*

Male and female have same pattern, but colours are different. Juveniles similar to females, but lacking black cap and grey nape. Note black tail and white rump. Feed in trees or on the ground. Breeds in all Europe except southern Spain.

Hawfinch *18 cm R*

Very large head and bill. White wing-bars noticeable in flight. Very wary and hard to watch. Often feeds on the ground, disappearing into cover when disturbed. Breeds sparsely in broad-leaved woodlands and orchards across Europe (not Ireland or Norway and rarely in Scotland or Wales).

Crossbill *16·5 cm RW*

May be difficult to see when feeding high in spruce or fir.

Note shape of bill. Often first noticed by metallic 'chip-chip' flight call. Normally breeds in conifer forests in Scottish Highlands, Scandinavia, eastern Europe, Spain and southern Italy.

Siskin *12 cm RSPW*

Small. Note double yellow wing-bars and yellow on tail (compare larger greenfinch, see page 165). Note also deep fork in tail. Feeds high in trees, especially alders and birches,

or on nuts in garden. Breeds in conifer and mixed woods in Scotland, Ireland, Scandinavia, Germany, Alps and Pyrenees. Winters in most of Europe.

Serin *11·5 cm*

Very small, greenish-yellow finch. Yellow rump. Longer-tailed than siskin. Juvenile very heavily streaked. Breeds in orchards, scrub, gardens and woodland edges across Europe (except British Isles and Scandinavia).

Golden oriole *24 cm P*

Slightly larger than starling. Yellow and black male hard to mistake unless seen in silhouette when it looks thrushlike. Female could be mistaken for green woodpecker, but shape entirely different. Flight undulating. Breeds in broadleaved woodland, parks and large gardens across Europe (occasionally southern England and southern Scandinavia).

Waxwing *18 cm W*

Note crest and stumpy tail. Only European bird with yellow-tipped tail. High-pitched, weak call. Breeds in open birch and conifer forests in far north of Scandinavia and Russia. Winters west across Europe including British Isles. Very plentiful in some years.

Starling *21·5 cm RW*

Shorter-tailed, smaller and more upright than blackbird. No yellow eye-ring. Immatures going into adult plumage have brown and iridescent plumage mixed. Rapid wing-beats in flight. Noisy and a good mimic. Breeds in woodlands and near human dwellings across Europe (except Spain, Sardinia, Corsica and Sicily where it is replaced by spotless starling).

Jay *34 cm R*

White rump, black tail and blue wing-flashes show clearly in rear view. Flies with slow wing action (like an oarsman). Noisy outside breeding season. Breeds in woods, large gardens and parks across Europe (not northern Scandinavia).

Nutcracker *32 cm*

Note white on, and under, tail, broad wings and long bill. Perches on top of trees. Breeds in Alps and eastern Scandinavia east to Russia in conifer forests.

Alpine Chough *38 cm*

Green-black rather than purple-black of chough. Plumage less glossy. Flight similar to chough. Breeds in rocky mountains from northern Spain to the Balkans.

Magpie *46 cm R*

Usually appears simply black and white. Long tail and bold marking very obvious on ground, more difficult to see in tops of bare trees. Weak, undulating flight. Note short tail of juvenile. Breeds all over Europe.

Chough *39·5 cm R*

May be confused with jackdaw which is smaller and less acrobatic in flight, and alpine chough. Wings in flight rather square-ended with noticeable 'fingers'. Breeds on steep cliffs and rock faces in north-west France, Ireland, Wales and western Scotland

Raven

Raven Carrion crow Rook Jackdaw

Carrion crow

imm.

Rook

Hooded crow

Jackdaw

juv.

(normally near sea), and inland in Spain and southern Mediterranean.

Raven *64 cm R*

Very heavy bill and shaggy throat. Head and wedge-shaped tail very noticeable in flight, also deeply fingered wings. Very acrobatic. Call a very deep croak. Widespread breeding in uplands of western British Isles, north-west France, Spain, Italy, Balkans and Scandinavia.

Carrion/hooded crow *47 cm R*

Two distinct races—carrion crow all black and hooded crow grey and black. Has greenish gloss rather than purple gloss of rook. Usually seen singly or in pairs. Call—rasping 'kaah'. Breeds in all types of country. Carrion crow breeds in western Europe except Ireland. Hooded crow breeds in Scandinavia, eastern Europe, Alps, Italy, northern Scotland and Ireland.

Rook *46 cm R*

Looks less compact in flight than carrion crow and is frequently seen in flocks. Call— 'caw'. Breeds in rookeries in trees in farmland across western Europe.

Jackdaw *33 cm R*

Note grey nape. Small with high pitched 'chack' call. Very jerky movements in flight and when walking. Widespread breeding across Europe in many habitats.

Wood pigeon

imm.

Stock dove

Rock dove

Turtle dove

imm.

Wood pigeon *41 cm RW*

Largest European pigeon. Note white collar, plum-coloured breast and, in flight, white wing-bars. Small head noticeable in silhouette. Flies hard and fast with deep chest often noticeable. Breeds across Europe, wintering in western Europe.

Stock dove *33 cm RW*

Smaller than wood pigeon with narrower, more pointed wings. Note black-tipped tail, black trailing edge to wing and no white plumage. Less obviously deep-chested in flight. Breeds in woodland, farmland with trees and parks, over most of Europe. Nests in holes in trees, cliffs and ruins.

Rock dove *33 cm R*

Note white rump, black tip to tail and double black wing-bar. Very pale underwing noticeable in flight. Breeds in northern Scotland, northern and western Ireland, north-west France, Spain and Mediterranean. Feral or town pigeon bred from rock doves, and shows many different plumage phases.

Collared dove

collared dove underview

turtle dove underview

imm.

juv. fostered by wren

Cuckoo

rufous phase

Turtle dove *27 cm S*

Note neck pattern, thin neck, white belly and chequered wing pattern and white tail markings. Very soft, purring 'coo' call. Immature lacks rosy breast and is dull brown. Breeds in open woodland, orchards, farmland across Europe (not Scandinavia and rarely Scotland).

Collared dove *32 cm R*

Larger and sturdier-looking than turtle dove. Note dark-tipped grey wings contrasting with brown back and thin black collar. From below most distinguishing mark is white and black tail pattern. Breeds across Europe in farmland and gardens, particularly near human habitation.

Cuckoo *33 cm SP*

Looks like falcon in flight. Lays eggs in other birds' nests. Sexes alike. Breeds in almost all habitats from moorland to coastal marshes throughout Europe.

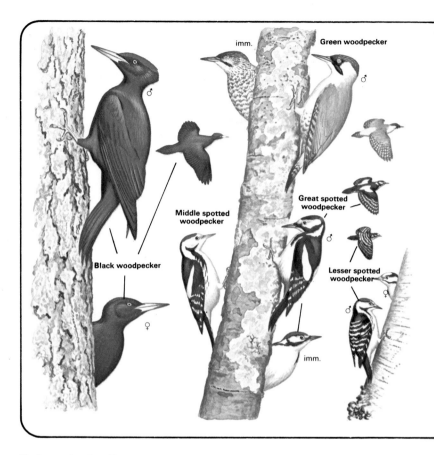

Black woodpecker

imm.

Green woodpecker

♂

Middle spotted woodpecker

Great spotted woodpecker

♂

Lesser spotted woodpecker

♂

♀

imm.

Black woodpecker *46 cm*

Totally black with red head (note difference between sexes). Head, often held back. Markedly undulating flight. Breeds in coniferous, mixed and beech woodland in Netherlands, Germany, Alps, central France, Pyrenees and north-west Spain.

Green woodpecker *32 cm R*

Often on grass feeding on ants. Loud, ringing call. Breeds in broad-leaved woodland, park-

land, gardens and roadside trees across Europe (not Scottish Highlands, Ireland or northern Scandinavia).

Middle spotted woodpecker *22 cm*

Breeds in broad-leaved and mixed woodland, parks and gardens west from north Spain across Europe (not Britain).

Great spotted woodpecker *23 cm R*

Note white wing-patches and

black head (see middle spotted woodpecker). In spring, drums with rapid blows for about a second. Breeds in woodland, parks, large gardens and roadside trees over most of Europe (not Ireland).

Lesser spotted woodpecker *14·5 cm R*

Sparrow-sized and more delicate than great spotted woodpecker. Drums more rapidly than great spotted and for longer (up to 30 blows in

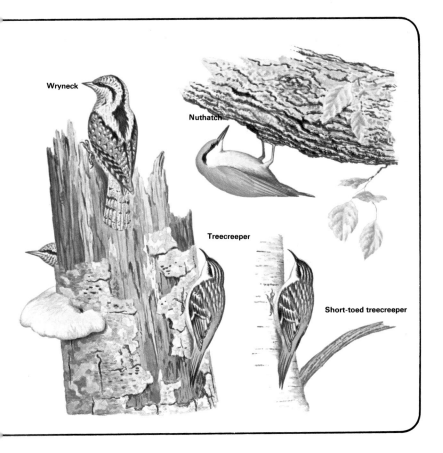

Wryneck

Nuthatch

Treecreeper

Short-toed treecreeper

2 seconds). Breeds in woodlands, parks and orchards
across Europe (not Ireland or
Scotland).

Wryneck *16·5 cm SP*

Square-ended, rather long tail.
Skulking, and hops on ground
with tail raised. Flight less
undulating and faster than
other woodpeckers. Breeds in
open broad-leaved woodlands,
orchards, and large gardens in
Europe (very rare in Britain but
seen on migration).

Nuthatch *14 cm R*

Climbs on tree bark going
downward head-first. Jerky
and flapping but fast flight.
Orange belly and underparts
noticeable in flight.
Breeds where there are trees
throughout Europe (not
Scotland, Ireland, northern
Scandinavia).

Treecreeper *12·5 cm R*

Creeps up trees, never down,
searching for insects and
looking rather like a pale

mouse. Breeds in conifer and
mixed woodlands in Europe,
east from France, and also in
broad-leaved woodland, parks
and gardens in British Isles.

Short-toed treecreeper
12·5 cm

Hard to distinguish from treecreeper but has brown flanks
and louder, less high-pitched
call. Breeds in Europe (not
British Isles or Scandinavia) in
broad-leaved woodland, parks
and gardens in lowland areas.

173

Goldcrest *9 cm RPW*

Very small. Tiny bill, golden
crest and olive back. No eye-
stripe. High-pitched song. Very
agile—often hanging on underside of branches. Breeds in
most of Europe, except parts of
Spain and Italy, in woods,
parks and large gardens,
especially with conifers.

Firecrest *9 cm RPW*

Similar to goldcrest. Note
black and white eye-stripes.
Breeds in habitat similar to
goldcrest's but no preference
for conifers. Breeds in southern
England (rare) and rest of
Europe except Scandinavia.

Spotted flycatcher *14 cm S*

Striped rather than spotted.
Sexes alike. Juvenile more
spotted. Perches upright.
Breeds in woodland edges,
parks and gardens across
Europe.

Pied flycatcher *13 cm S*

Both sexes have white outer
tail feathers. Breeds broad-
leaved woodland in western
British Isles, Scandinavia,
Spain and eastwards from
France.

Dunnock *14·5 cm RP*

Greyish brown appearance.
Skulking; feeds on the ground.
Sexes alike. Juvenile rather
brown like meadow pipit.
Displays by flapping wing very
fast. Breeds in undergrowth in
gardens, commons, parks and
woodland throughout Europe.

Black redstart ♂

Redstart ♂

♀

♀

imm.

Wren

Robin

Nightingale

imm.

imm.

Black redstart *14 cm SP*

Females very similar to female redstarts, but duskier and with less red on rump. Breeds on rocky hills, mountains, cliffs, villages and towns, often using houses for nesting. Breeds in southern and eastern England (rare), rest of Europe except Scandinavia.

Redstart *14 cm S*

Note amount of russet on tail of female. Compare with female black redstart. Breeds in woodland and gardens in Europe (not Ireland).

Wren *9·5 cm R*

Very small with eye-stripe, and upright, pointed tail. Rather mouse-like when feeding along foot of fence or hedge. Sings very loudly from prominent perch. Breeds throughout Europe except northern Scandinavia.

Robin *14 cm RSPW*

Male and female alike. Song is a warbling scolding 'tic-tic' call. Breeds in forests, gardens and parks across Europe. Rather shy except in British Isles.

Nightingale *16·5 cm S*

Larger than robin but brown with reddish tail. Skulking. Flies low between cover. Juvenile like large juvenile robin. Rich song with 'jug-jug' call note. Breeds in England (south from Humber river), rest of Europe except Scandinavia.

Long-tailed tit

imm.

Coal tit

imm.

Blue tit

imm.

Long-tailed tit *14 cm R*

Tail longer than body. Very small. Weak flyer, flits from tree to tree. Often in family parties. Breeds in woodland, commons, large gardens and parks across Europe.

Coal tit *11·5 cm R*

Note white nape. Black head and white cheeks. Body grey-brown. Juvenile yellowish. Often feeds on ground. Breeds in woodland (conifer and mixed), parks and gardens across Europe.

Blue tit *11·5 cm R*

Note blue head and tail. Juvenile has yellowish cheeks and is less blue. Breeds in broad-leaved woodland, parks, gardens and hedgerows across Europe except Scandinavia.

Great tit *14 cm R*

Largest tit. Black head, white cheeks, broad black band down breast (broader in male than female). Various songs, best-known sounds like 'teacher-teacher'. Breeds in broad-leaved woodland, gardens, parks and hedgerows across Europe.

Great tit

imm.

Crested tit

Marsh tit

Willow tit

Crested tit *11·5 cm R*

Note crest. No wing-bars. Trilling song and hissing contact note similar to coal tit. Breeds in conifer and mixed woodland across Europe (not Ireland, England, Wales or Italy).

Marsh tit *11·5 cm R*

Totally black crown and nape. Glossy black crown. No pale wing-patch. Call–'pitchoo' and scolding 'chick-adee-dee-dee'. Breeds in broad-leaved woodland and scrub across Europe (not Ireland or Scotland).

Willow tit *11·5 cm R*

Very similar to marsh tit but with pale wing-patch and matt black head. Grating nasal and wheezy calls. Juveniles almost impossible to separate from juvenile marsh tit. Breeds in Europe (not Ireland, Spain or Italy).

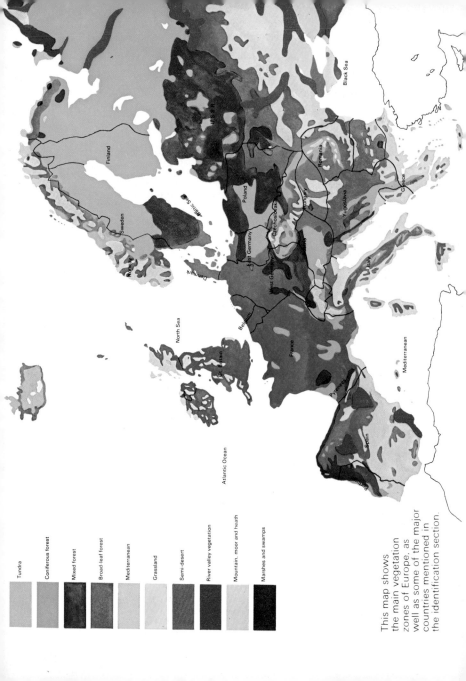

Tundra

Coniferous forest

Mixed forest

Broad-leaf forest

Mediterranean

Grassland

Semi-desert

River valley vegetation

Mountain, moor and heath

Marshes and swamps

This map shows
the main vegetation
zones of Europe, as
well as some of the major
countries mentioned in
the identification section.

U.S.S.R.

Finland

Sweden

Norway

Baltic Sea

Denmark

North Sea

Gt. Britain

Atlantic Ocean

East Germany

West Germany

Belgium

France

Poland

Czechoslovakia

Austria

Hungary

Romania

Yugoslavia

Italy

Greece

Black Sea

Pyrenees

Spain

Mediterranean

Checklist of European Birds

This list contains most of the species recorded in Europe. Some are rarely seen, but the most common have been included in our recognition guide. The order in which the families are listed follows J. L. Peters' list in *Check-list of the Birds of the World*. This is the sequence most commonly used by ornithologists, and it starts with the most primitive families.

The list is divided into groups, the largest of which are the *orders*. The orders are made up of *families*. From these you can see how closely related any two species are. Taxonomists – scientists who classify animals – use additional divisions such as *sub-orders* and *sub-families*, but we have left these out to prevent the list from becoming very complicated.

Each species has two scientific names. The first, which is always written with a capital initial, is the generic name, and from it you can see to which genus the species belongs. The second is the specific name and this denotes the species. Where there is a sub-species, a third scientific name is given and this indicates the race. We have not noted sub-species, except where they are particularly noticeable: for instance, the carrion crow and hooded crow.

Order Gaviiformes
Family Gaviidae
Red-throated diver *Gavia stellata*
Black-throated diver *Gavia arctica*
Great northern diver *Gavia immer*
White-billed diver *Gavia adamsii*

Order Podicipediformes
Family Podicipitidae
Little grebe *Tachybaptus ruficollis*
Black-necked grebe *Podiceps nigricollis*
Slavonian grebe *Podiceps auritus*
Red-necked grebe *Podiceps grisegena*
Great-crested grebe *Podiceps cristatus*

Order Procellariiformes
Family Procellariidae
Fulmar *Fulmarus glacialis*
Cory's shearwater *Calonectris diomedea*
Great shearwater *Puffinus gravis*
Sooty shearwater *Puffinus griseus*
Manx shearwater *Puffinus puffinus*
Little shearwater *Puffinus assimilus*

Family Hydrobatidae
Storm petrel *Hydrobates pelagicus*
Wilson's petrel *Oceanites oceanicus*
Leach's petrel *Oceanodroma leucorhoa*

Order Pelecaniformes
Family Pelecanidae
White pelican *Pelecanus onocrotalus*
Dalmatian pelican *Pelecanus crispus*

Family Sulidae
Gannet *Sula bassana*
Family Phalacrocoracidae
Cormorant *Phalacrocorax carbo*
Shag *Phalacrocorax aristotelis*
Pygmy cormorant *Phalacrocorax pygmeus*

Order Ciconiiformes
Family Ardeidae
Bittern *Botaurus stellaris*
American bittern *Botaurus lentiginosus*
Little bittern *Ixobrychus minutus*
Night heron *Nycticorax nycticorax*
Squacco heron *Ardeola ralloides*
Cattle egret *Bubulcus ibis*

Great white egret *Egretta alba*
Little egret *Egretta garzetta*
Grey heron *Ardea cinerea*
Purple heron *Ardea purpurea*
Family Ciconiidae
White stork *Ciconia ciconia*
Black stork *Ciconia nigra*
Family Threskiornithidae
Spoonbill *Platalea leucorodia*
Glossy ibis *Plegadis falcinellus*
Family Phoenicopteridae
Greater flamingo *Phoenicopterus ruber*

Order Anseriformes
Family Anatidae

Canada goose *Branta canadensis*
Barnacle goose *Branta leucopsis*
Brent goose *Branta bernicla*
Red-breasted goose *Branta ruficollis*
Greylag goose *Anser anser*
White-fronted goose *Anser albifrons*
Lesser white-fronted goose *Anser erythropus*
Bean goose *Anser fabalis*
Pink-footed goose *Anser brachyrhynchus*
Snow goose *Anser caerulescens*
Mute swan *Cygnus olor*
Whooper swan *Cygnus cygnus*
Bewick's swan *Cygnus bewickii*
Ruddy shelduck *Tadorna ferruginea*
Shelduck *Tadorna tadorna*
Mallard *Anas platyrhynchos*
Teal *Anas crecca*
Blue-winged teal *Anas discors*
Baikal teal *Anas formosa*
Gadwall *Anas strepera*
Wigeon *Anas penelope*
American wigeon *Anas americana*
Pintail *Anas acuta*
Garganey *Anas querquedula*
Shoveler *Anas clypeata*
Marbled teal *Anas angustirostris*
Red-crested pochard *Netta rufina*
Pochard *Aythya ferina*
Ferruginous duck *Aythya nyroca*
Tufted duck *Aythya fuligula*
Scaup *Aythya marila*
Mandarin duck *Aix galericulata*
Eider *Somateria mollissima*
King eider *Somateria spectabilis*
Steller's eider *Polysticta stelleri*
Common scoter *Melanitta nigra*
Velvet scoter *Melanitta fusca*
Surf scoter *Melanitta perspicillata*
Harlequin duck *Histrionicus histrionicus*
Long-tailed duck *Clangula hyemalis*
Goldeneye *Bucephala clangula*

Barrow's goldeneye *Bucephala islandica*
Smew *Mergus albellus*
Red-breasted merganser *Mergus serrator*
Goosander *Mergus merganser*
White-headed duck *Oxyura leucocephala*

Order Falconiformes
Family Pandionidae

Osprey *Pandion haliaetus*

Family Accipitridae
Black-winged kite *Elanus caeruleus*
Honey buzzard *Pernis apivorus*
Red kite *Milvus milvus*
Black kite *Milvus migrans*
Goshawk *Accipiter gentilis*
Levant sparrowhawk *Accipiter brevipes*
Sparrowhawk *Accipiter nisus*
Rough-legged buzzard *Buteo lagopus*
Long-legged buzzard *Buteo rufinus*
Buzzard *Buteo buteo*
Booted eagle *Hieraeetus pennatus*
Bonelli's eagle *Hieraeetus fasciatus*
Tawny eagle *Aquila rapax*
Spotted eagle *Aquila clanga*
Lesser spotted eagle *Aquila pomarina*
Imperial eagle *Aquila heliaca*
Golden eagle *Aquila chrysaetos*
White-tailed eagle *Haliaetus albicilla*
Short-toed eagle *Circaetus gallicus*
Hen harrier *Circus cyaneus*
Pallid harrier *Circus macrourus*
Montagu's harrier *Circus pygargus*
Marsh harrier *Circus aeruginosus*
Egyptian vulture *Neophron percnopterus*
Bearded vulture *Gypaetus barbatus*
Black vulture *Aegypius monachus*
Griffon vulture *Gyps fulvus*
Family Falconidae
Gyr falcon *Falco rusticolus*
Saker *Falco cherrug*
Lanner *Falco biarmicus*
Peregrine *Falco peregrinus*
Hobby *Falco subbuteo*
Eleonora's falcon *Falco eleonorae*
Merlin *Falco columbarius*
Red-footed falcon *Falco vespertinus*
Lesser kestrel *Falco naumanni*
Kestrel *Falco tinnunculus*

Order Galliformes
Family Tetraonidae

Willow grouse *Lagopus lagopus lagopus*
Red grouse *Lagopus lagopus scoticus*
Ptarmigan *Lagopus mutus*
Hazel hen *Tetrastes bonasia*
Black grouse *Lyrurus tetrix*

Capercaillie *Tetrao urogallus*
Family Phasianidae
Rock Partridge *Alectoris graeca*
Chukar *Alectoris chukar*
Barbary partridge *Alectoris barbara*
Red-legged partridge *Alectoris rufa*
Partridge *Perdix perdix*
Quail *Coturnix coturnix*
Pheasant *Phasianus colchicus*

Order Gruiformes
Family Gruidae
Andalusian hemipode *Turnix sylvatica*
Crane *Grus grus*
Demoiselle crane *Anthropoides virgo*
Family Rallidae
Water rail *Rallus aquaticus*
Spotted crake *Porzana porzana*
Little crake *Porzana parva*
Baillon's crake *Porzana pusilla*
Corncrake *Crex crex*
Moorhen *Gallinula chloropus*
Purple gallinule *Porphyrio porphyrio*
Coot *Fulica atra*
Crested coot *Fulica cristata*
Family Otididae
Great bustard *Otis tarda*
Little bustard *Otis tetrax*
Houbara bustard *Chlamydotis undulata*

Order Charadriiformes
Family Haematopodidae
Oystercatcher *Haematopus ostralegus*
Family Charadriidae
Ringed plover *Charadrius hiaticula*
Little ringed plover *Charadrius dubius*
Kentish plover *Charadrius alexandrinus*
Greater sandplover *Charadrius leschenaultii*
Dotterel *Eudromias morinellus*
Golden plover *Pluvialis apricaria*
Lesser golden plover *Pluvialis dominica*
Grey plover *Pluvialis squatarola*
Killdeer *Charadrius vociferus*
Sociable plover *Vanellus gregarius*
Lapwing *Vanellus vanellus*
Spur-winged plover *Vanellus spinosus*
Turnstone *Arenaria interpres*
Family Scolopacidae
Little stint *Calidris minuta*
Temminck's stint *Calidris temminckii*
White-rumped sandpiper *Calidris fuscicollis*
Sharp-tailed sandpiper *Calidris acuminata*
Pectoral sandpiper *Calidris melanotos*
Semi-palmated sandpiper *Calidris pusilla*
Purple sandpiper *Calidris maritima*
Dunlin *Calidris alpina*

Curlew sandpiper *Calidris ferruginea*
Knot *Calidris canutus*
Sanderling *Calidris alba*
Ruff *Philomachus pugnax*
Buff-breasted sandpiper *Tryngites subruficollis*
Broad-billed sandpiper *Limicola falcinellus*
Long-billed dowitcher *Limnodromus scolopaceus*
Spotted redshank *Tringa erythropus*
Redshank *Tringa totanus*
Solitary sandpiper *Tringa solitaria*
Marsh sandpiper *Tringa stagnatilis*
Greenshank *Tringa nebularia*
Greater yellowlegs *Tringa melanoleuca*
Lesser yellowlegs *Tringa flavipes*
Green sandpiper *Tringa ochropus*
Wood sandpiper *Tringa glareola*
Common sandpiper *Tringa hypoleucos*
Spotted sandpiper *Tringa macularia*
Terek sandpiper *Tringa cinereus*
Black-tailed godwit *Limosa limosa*
Bar-tailed godwit *Limosa lapponica*
Curlew *Numenius arquata*
Slender-billed curlew *Numenius tenuirostris*
Whimbrel *Numenius phaeopus*
Upland sandpiper *Bartramia longicauda*
Woodcock *Scolopax rusticola*
Snipe *Gallinago gallinago*
Great snipe *Gallinago media*
Jack snipe *Lymnocryptes minimus*
Family Recurvirostridae
Black-winged stilt *Himantopus himantopus*
Avocet *Recurvirostra avosetta*
Family Phalaropodidae
Grey phalarope *Phalaropus fulicarius*
Red-necked phalarope *Phalaropus lobatus*
Wilson's phalarope *Phalaropus tricolor*
Family Burhinidae
Stone curlew *Burhinus oedicnemus*
Family Glareolidae
Cream-coloured courser *Cursorius cursor*
Pratincole *Glareola pratincola*
Black-winged pratincole *Glareola nordmanni*
Family Stercorariidae
Great skua *Stercorarius skua*
Pomarine skua *Stercorarius pomarinus*
Arctic skua *Stercorarius parasiticus*
Long-tailed skua *Stercorarius longicaudus*
Family Laridae
Mediterranean gull *Larus melanocephalus*
Bonaparte's gull *Larus philadelphia*
Little gull *Larus minutus*
Black-headed gull *Larus ridibundus*
Slender-billed gull *Larus genei*
Lesser black-backed gull *Larus fuscus*
Herring gull *Larus argentatus*

Iceland gull *Larus glaucoides*
Glaucous gull *Larus hyperboreus*
Great black-backed gull *Larus marinus*
Common gull *Larus canus*
Audouin's gull *Larus audouinii*
Sabine's gull *Larus sabini*
Kittiwake *Rissa tridactyla*
Ross's gull *Rhodostethia rosea*
Ivory gull *Pagophila eburnea*
Black tern *Chlidonias niger*
White-winged black tern *Chlidonias
    leucopterus*
Whiskered tern *Chlidonias hybrida*
Gull-billed tern *Gelochelidon nilotica*
Caspian tern *Hydroprogne caspia*
Sandwich tern *Sterna sandvicensis*
Common tern *Sterna hirundo*
Arctic tern *Sterna paradisaea*
Roseate tern *Sterna dougallii*
Sooty tern *Sterna fuscata*
Little tern *Sterna albifrons*
Family Alcidae
Little auk *Alle alle*
Razorbill *Alca torda*
Guillemot *Uria aalge*
Brünnich's guillemot *Uria lomvia*
Black guillemot *Cepphus grylle*
Puffin *Fratercula arctica*

Order Columbiformes
Family Pteroclididae
Black-bellied sandgrouse *Pterocles orientalis*
Pin-tailed sandgrouse *Pterocles alchata*
Pallas's sandgrouse *Syrrhaptes paradoxus*

Family Columbidae
Wood pigeon *Columba palumbus*
Stock dove *Columba oenas*
Rock dove *Columba livia*
Collared dove *Streptopelia decaocto*
Palm dove *Streptopelia senegalensis*
Turtle dove *Streptopelia turtur*

Order Cuculiformes
Family Cuculidae
Cuckoo *Cuculus canorus*
Great spotted cuckoo *Clamator glandarius*
Yellow-billed cuckoo *Coccyzus americanus*
Black-billed cuckoo *Coccyzus erythropthalmus*

Order Strigiformes
Family Tytonidae
Barn owl *Tyto alba*

Family Strigidae
Snowy owl *Nyctea scandiaca*

Eagle owl *Bubo bubo*
Long-eared owl *Asio otus*
Short-eared owl *Asio flammeus*
Scops owl *Otus scops*
Tengmalm's owl *Aegolius funereus*
Little owl *Athene noctua*
Pygmy owl *Glaucidium passerinum*
Hawk owl *Surnia ulula*
Tawny owl *Strix aluco*
Ural owl *Strix uralensis*
Great grey owl *Strix nebulosa*

Order Caprimulgiformes
Family Caprimulgidae
Nightjar *Caprimulgus europaeus*
Red-necked nightjar *Caprimulgus ruficollis*
Egyptian nightjar *Caprimulgus aegyptius*

Order Apodiformes
Family Apodidae
Pallid swift *Apus pallidus*
Swift *Apus apus*
Alpine swift *Apus melba*

Order Coraciiformes
Family Alcedinidae
Kingfisher *Alcedo atthis*
Family Meropidae
Bee-eater *Merops apiaster*
Family Coraciidae
Roller *Coracias garrulus*
Family Upupidae
Hoopoe *Upupa epops*

Order Piciformes
Family Picidae
Wryneck *Jynx torquilla*
Green woodpecker *Picus viridis*
Grey-headed woodpecker *Picus canus*
Black woodpecker *Dryocopus martius*
Great spotted woodpecker *Dendrocopos
    major*
Syrian woodpecker *Dendrocopos syriacus*
Middle spotted woodpecker *Dendrocopos
    medius*
White-backed woodpecker *Dendrocopos
    leucotos*
Lesser spotted woodpecker *Dendrocopos
    minor*
Three-toed woodpecker *Picoides tridactylus*

Order Passeriformes
Family Alaudidae
Dupont's lark *Chersophilus duponti*

Short-toed lark *Calandrella cinerea*
Lesser short-toed lark *Calandrella rufescens*
Calandra lark *Melanocorypha calandra*
White-winged lark *Melanocorypha leucoptera*
Black lark *Melanocorypha yeltoniensis*
Shore lark *Eremophila alpestris*
Crested lark *Galerida cristata*
Thekla lark *Galerida theklae*
Woodlark *Lullula arborea*
Skylark *Alauda arvensis*
Family Hirundinidae
Sand martin *Riparia riparia*
Crag martin *Hirundo rupestris*
Swallow *Hirundo rustica*
Red-rumped swallow *Hirundo daurica*
House martin *Delichon urbica*
Family Motacillidae
Richard's pipit *Anthus novaeseelandiae*
Tawny pipit *Anthus campestris*
Tree pipit *Anthus trivialis*
Pechora pipit *Anthus gustavi*
Meadow pipit *Anthus pratensis*
Red-throated pipit *Anthus cervinus*
Water/Rock pipit *Anthus spinoletta*
Yellow wagtail *Motacilla flava*
Grey wagtail *Motacilla cinerea*
Pied/White wagtail *Motacilla alba*
Citrine wagtail *Motacilla citreola*
Family Laniidae
Red-backed shrike *Lanius collurio*
Masked shrike *Lanius nubicus*
Woodchat shrike *Lanius senator*
Lesser grey shrike *Lanius minor*
Great grey shrike *Lanius excubitor*
Family Bombycillidae
Waxwing *Bombycilla garrulus*
Family Cinclidae
Dipper *Cinclus cinclus*
Family Troglodytidae
Wren *Troglodytes troglodytes*
Family Prunellidae
Alpine accentor *Prunella collaris*
Dunnock *Prunella modularis*
Family Muscicapidae
Cetti's warbler *Cettia cetti*
Savi's warbler *Locustella luscinioides*
River warbler *Locustella fluviatilis*
Pallas's grasshopper warbler *Locustella certhiola*
Grasshopper warbler *Locustella naevia*
Lanceolated warbler *Locustella lanceolata*
Moustached warbler *Acrocephalus melanopogon*
Aquatic warbler *Acrocephalus paludicola*
Sedge warbler *Acrocephalus schoenobaenus*
Blyth's reed warbler *Acrocephalus dumetorum*

Marsh warbler *Acrocephalus palustris*
Reed warbler *Acrocephalus scirpaceus*
Great reed warbler *Acrocephalus arundinaceus*
Icterine warbler *Hippolais icterina*
Melodious warbler *Hippolais polyglotta*
Olive-tree warbler *Hippolais olivetorum*
Olivaceous warbler *Hippolais pallida*
Barred warbler *Sylvia nisoria*
Orphean warbler *Sylvia hortensis*
Garden warbler *Sylvia borin*
Blackcap *Sylvia atricapilla*
Whitethroat *Sylvia communis*
Lesser whitethroat *Sylvia curruca*
Rüppell's warbler *Sylvia ruppelli*
Sardinian warbler *Sylvia melanocephala*
Subalpine warbler *Sylvia cantillans*
Spectacled warbler *Sylvia conspicillata*
Dartford warbler *Sylvia undata*
Marmora's warbler *Sylvia sarda*
Willow warbler *Phylloscopus trochilus*
Chiffchaff *Phylloscopus collybita*
Bonelli's warbler *Phylloscopus bonelli*
Wood warbler *Phylloscopus sibilatrix*
Yellow-browed warbler *Phylloscopus inornatus*
Pallas's warbler *Phylloscopus proregulus*
Arctic warbler *Phylloscopus borealis*
Greenish warbler *Phylloscopus trochiloides*
Goldcrest *Regulus regulus*
Firecrest *Regulus ignicapillus*
Fan-tailed warbler *Cisticola juncidis*
Pied flycatcher *Ficedula hypoleuca*
Collared flycatcher *Ficedula albicollis*
Red-breasted flycatcher *Ficedula parva*
Spotted flycatcher *Muscicapa striata*
Whinchat *Saxicola rubetra*
Stonechat *Saxicola torquata*
Wheatear *Oenanthe oenanthe*
Pied wheatear *Oenanthe pleschanka*
Black-eared wheatear *Oenanthe hispanica*
Desert wheatear *Oenanthe deserti*
Isabelline wheatear *Oenanthe isabellina*
Black wheatear *Oenanthe leucura*
Rufous bushchat *Cercotrichas galactotes*
Rock thrush *Monticola saxatilis*
Blue rock thrush *Monticola solitarius*
Black redstart *Phoenicurus ochruros*
Redstart *Phoenicurus phoenicurus*
Robin *Erithacus rubecula*
Nightingale *Luscinia megarhynchos*
Thrush nightingale *Luscinia luscinia*
Bluethroat *Luscinia svecica*
Red-flanked bluetail *Tarsiger cyanurus*
Olive-backed thrush *Catharus ustulatus*
Eye-browed thrush *Turdus obscurus*
Black-throated thrush *Turdus ruficollis*

Dusky thrush *Turdus naumanni*
Fieldfare *Turdus pilaris*
Ring ouzel *Turdus torquatus*
American robin *Turdus migratorius*
Blackbird *Turdus merula*
Siberian thrush *Turdus sibiricus*
Redwing *Turdus iliacus*
Song thrush *Turdus philomelos*
Mistle thrush *Turdus viscivorus*
White's thrush *Zoothera dauma*
Bearded tit *Panurus biarmicus*

Family Aegithalidae
Long-tailed tit *Aegithelos caudatus*

Family Paridae
Marsh tit *Parus palustris*
Willow tit *Parus montanus*
Sombre tit *Parus lugubris*
Siberian tit *Parus cinctus*
Crested tit *Parus cristatus*
Coal tit *Parus ater*
Blue tit *Parus caeruleus*
Azure tit *Parus cyanus*
Great tit *Parus major*

Family Remizidae
Penduline tit *Remiz pendulinus*

Family Sittidae
Nuthatch *Sitta europaea*
Corsican nuthatch *Sitta whiteheadi*
Rock nuthatch *Sitta neumayer*
Wall creeper *Tichodroma muraria*

Family Certhiidae
Treecreeper *Certhia familiaris*
Short-toed tree creeper *Certhia brachydactyla*

Family Emberizidae
Corn bunting *Emberiza calandra*
Yellowhammer *Emberiza citrinella*
Rock bunting *Emberiza cia*
Cinereous bunting *Emberiza cineracea*
Ortolan bunting *Emberiza hortulana*
Cretzschmar's bunting *Emberiza caesia*
Cirl bunting *Emberiza cirlus*
Little bunting *Emberiza pusilla*
Rustic bunting *Emberiza rustica*
Yellow-breasted bunting *Emberiza aureola*
Black-headed bunting *Emberiza
melanocephala*
Reed bunting *Emberiza schoeniclus*

Lapland bunting *Calcarius lapponicus*
Snow bunting *Plectrophenax nivalis*

Family Fringillidae
Chaffinch *Fringilla coelebs*
Brambling *Fringilla montifringilla*
Citril finch *Serinus citrinella*
Serin *Serinus serinus*
Greenfinch *Carduelis chloris*
Siskin *Carduelis spinus*
Goldfinch *Carduelis carduelis*
Twite *Acanthis flavirostris*
Linnet *Acanthis cannabina*
Redpoll *Acanthis flammea*
Arctic redpoll *Acanthus hornemanni*
Trumpeter bullfinch *Rhodopechys githaginea*
Scarlet rosefinch *Carpodacus erythrinus*
Pine grosbeak *Pinicola enucleator*
Parrot crossbill *Loxia pytyopsittacus*
Crossbill *Loxia curvirostra*
Two-barred crossbill *Loxia leucoptera*
Bullfinch *Pyrrhula pyrrhula*
Hawfinch *Coccothraustes coccothraustes*

Family Ploceidae
House sparrow *Passer domesticus*
Spanish sparrow *Passer hispaniolensis*
Tree sparrow *Passer montanus*
Rock sparrow *Petronia petronia*
Snow finch *Montifringilla nivalis*

Family Sturnidae
Rose-coloured starling *Sturnus roseus*
Starling *Sturnus vulgaris*
Spotless starling *Sturnus unicolor*

Family Oriolidae
Golden oriole *Oriolus oriolus*

Family Corvidae
Siberian jay *Perisoreus infaustus*
Jay *Garrulus glandarius*
Azure-winged magpie *Cyanopica cyanus*
Magpie *Pica pica*
Nutcracker *Nucifraga caryocatactes*
Chough *Pyrrhocorax pyrrhocorax*
Alpine chough *Pyrrhocorax graculus*
Jackdaw *Corvus monedula*
Rook *Corvus frugilegus*
Hooded/Carrion crow *Corvus corone*
Raven *Corvus corax*

Building up a Birdwatcher's Library

Bird books can be found in every bookshop, but it can be quite a problem deciding which to buy. The following lists will help you decide which you need.

Identification Books

The Hamlyn Guide to Birds of Britain and Europe by Bertel Bruun and Arthur Singer (Hamlyn); *A Field Guide to the Birds of Britain and Europe* by Roger Tory Peterson, Guy Mountford, and P. A. D. Hollom (Collins); and *The Birds of Britain and Europe* by Hermann Heinzel, Richard Fitter and John Parslow (Collins). Because these three cover a large area, and many species, the beginner may like to start with *The RSPB Guide to British Birds* by David Saunders (Hamlyn), which deals with 200 of the most common British birds.

Reference Books

Two reference books which will be particularly helpful to the young birdwatcher are *The Birdlife of Britain* by Peter Hayman and Philip Burton (Mitchell Beazley in association with RSPB) and *The Popular Handbook of British Birds* by P. A. D. Hollom (Witherby). They are both invaluable; the first because it includes illustrations of many aspects of birds, and the sec-

ond because it contains much basic information about them.

The distribution of birds is the subject of a very interesting reference book called *The Atlas of Breeding Birds in Britain and Ireland* by J. T. R. Sharrock (British Trust for Ornithology and Irish Wildbird Conservancy). This book shows where species breed in the British Isles. Similar atlases have now been published in other European countries.

Other Books

Your choice of books on other aspects of birds will depend on your particular interests, but the following publishers specialise in natural history books.

The Hamlyn Group, Feltham, Middlesex, have built up a large list of well produced, highly illustrated books on natural history, particularly birds.

Collins publish field guides on many subjects. The 'New Naturalist' series is also published by Collins.

David & Charles of Newton Abbott, Devon, and T. & A. D. Poyser of Berkhamstead, Hertfordshire, have both published a number of very good bird books.

Several other publishers produce bird books, and your local bookshop should stock most titles.

Organisations to Join

Learning about birds from books is useful, but learning from expert ornithologists is much more effective. You can meet such people through local bird clubs or natural history societies, details of which you can obtain from your local library, or by joining the Young Ornithologists' Club. This is the national club for birdwatchers of fifteen years and under.

The YOC is part of the Royal Society for the Protection of Birds (RSPB), Europe's leading bird conservation society. YOC members have their own twice-yearly magazine, in which there is information about birds and birdwatching, competitions, projects to take part in, and articles by YOC members. The YOC organises a number of other activities such as outings and holiday courses. Many local YOC groups share activities with the local RSPB members' groups so that young members have the opportunity to learn from experienced birdwatchers.

The RSPB also works closely with the British Trust for Ornithology, the national organisation for the amateur study of birds. The minimum age for members is fifteen years.

For details of the YOC and the RSPB, write to RSPB, The Lodge, Sandy, Bedfordshire SG19 2DL. For information about the BTO, write to BTO, Beech Grove, Tring, Hertfordshire.

Glossary

Accidental Bird which occurs in a particular place accidentally, due to storms, cloud and other adverse weather conditions. Also called vagrant.

Adaptive radiation The process through which a species adapts, and increases variety, to make the best use of its habitat.

Aerofoil Structure easily kept airborne, such as the wing of a bird or glider.

Aggression display The way in which a male bird protects its chosen breeding territory by threatening other males.

Alarm call Call from one bird to another to indicate the approach of danger.

Altricial Species which, on hatching, are blind, have little or no down and rely on their parents for both food and warmth.

Anting A form of feather care, during which the bird picks up ants and puts them in its plumage or flops down and allows the ants to crawl into the feathers. It is thought that the formic acid produced by the ants destroys or discourages feather-lice.

Aposematic colouring Warning colouring of some creatures which indicates that they are unpleasant tasting.

Ball-nest Enclosed ball-shaped nest.

Barbs Branches from the quill or rachis of the feather. Also called a 'ramus'.

Barbules Small hooks on a feather holding the vanes at the correct angle and in the right direction.

Bathing Method of feather care performed by dunking the underparts, throat and neck into the water.

Bill Horny extension of the jaw.

Binocular vision Seeing and focussing with both eyes at once, as do birds of prey.

Bird of prey Bird with talons and hooked bill. Members of the orders Falconiformes and Strigiformes.

Breeding plumage Distinctive plumage of a bird in the breeding season. Also called nuptial plumage'.

Bristle Small, sensory feathers around the bills of some species.

Brood (*Noun*) the young hatched from a single clutch of eggs. (*Verb*) to keep eggs or young birds warm.

Brood-parasite Bird which lays its eggs in other birds' nests, e.g. the cuckoo.

Brood-patch Feather-less area on the underside of the body where the skin is thickened with blood vessels to warm the eggs during incubation.

Camouflage Colouring, pattern or shape which helps an animal blend in with its surroundings so that it is not easily seen by its predators.

Carrion Carcases of animals, eaten by some species but not killed by them.

Chick Describes a bird until it is full-grown and able to fly. Also called a 'pullus' and 'nestling'.

Class Major group of animals such as fish, amphibians, reptiles, birds and mammals.

Cloaca An opening in the body of a bird, through which it passes waste material. During copulation the sperm is passed from the male's cloaca to the female's. The eggs pass out of the female's body through the cloaca.

Clutch Set of eggs laid by one female and brooded together.

Cock Male bird.

Cock-nest Nest made by a male bird.

Colony Large number of birds breeding together. Also applies to the location and the nests. Many seabirds nest in colonies.

Cones Colour-sensitive parts of the eye.

Contour Stiff feather which gives the bird its shape.

Convergent evolution Development of two different species in a similar way as a result of their having a similar habitat or environment.

Copulation Act of mating.

Corvid Member of the crow family or Corvidae.

Courtship Ritual pre-mating display. Also called the 'nuptial display'.

Courtship feeding Part of the ritual pre-mating display between some species, during which the male (in most cases) feeds the female.

Courtship preening Part of the ritual pre-mating display between some species. It consists of first one bird and then the other preening the head and nape of its mate.

Crepuscular Active at twilight.

Cryptic colouring Camouflage.

Cup-nest Hemispherical nest open at the top.

Dead ground Ground behind cover from which a birdwatcher cannot be seen by the birds he is watching.

Disruptive colouring Colouring which breaks up the outline of a bird so that it blends with its background.

Diurnal Active during daylight.

Down Very fine feathers which help to trap air and keep the bird warm.

Drag Resistance of air in flight.

Dusting Method of feather care by which fine dry earth, sand, and so on, is spread into the plumage by flicking movements of the wings. Thought to be a way of dislodging parasites.

Eclipse Moult which ducks undergo during the latter part of the summer.

Ecological niche Place within a total community which a particular species occupies.

Ecology Study of plants and animals in relation to their environment.

Ethology Study of animal behaviour.

Faecal sac Tiny transparent bag in which the droppings of young birds are produced.

Faeces Solid waste matter from the body.

Family One of the taxonomic groups by which animals are classified. There may be several genera in the same family and several families may make up an order.

Filoplume Small, fine feather found at the base of a contour feather.

First winter plumage Feathers a young bird grows in its first autumn moult, replacing the juvenile plumage.

Fledged Young birds are said to have 'fledged' when they can fly and have left the nest.

Follicle Cavity in a bird's skin out of which a feather grows.

Gamebird Bird from the order 'Galliformes' or any species which is hunted.

Gape Large, open mouth of a nestling which stimulates the parent to fill it with food.

Generic name The first of the scientific names of a species; given a capital initial. It is followed by the specific name.

Genus (plural Genera) A taxonomic group

by which animals are classified. Species are grouped in a genus, which may be one of several genera in a family.

Gizzard Second or muscular stomach of a bird, in which the food is ground after being mixed with gastric juices in the first stomach.

Habitat Place where a creature lives.

Habituation One type of learning ability, viz. the response to a repeated situation. For example, learning that certain animals are harmless.

Herbicide Chemical used in farming to kill unwanted plant pests, some of which have a harmful effect on birds.

Hirundine A member of the family Hirundidae – swallows and martins.

Immature Young bird which has passed the 'nestling' stage but has not yet reached full adulthood.

Imprinting Learning by being exposed to a situation at a very early age. For example, geese hatched in an incubator become fixated or 'imprinted' on humans and follow them about as they would a parent bird.

Incubate To sit on eggs so that they keep warm and hatch.

Insecticide Chemical used to kill insects.

Insight learning Perhaps the nearest ability to intelligence by which a bird can solve its problems, such as nest building, without having to use 'trial and error'.

Invertebrate Animal without a backbone (spinal column).

Jizz Birdwatcher's term for the combination of shape and movement by which a bird may be identified.

Juvenile Young bird which has its first real feathers after it has passed the 'nestling' stage and before it is described as an 'immature'.

Juvenile plumage Young bird's first feathers which push out the natal down. They are replaced in the autumn of the first year by the bird's first winter plumage.

Learning ability Degree to which a creature can gain knowledge from experience. Primitive bird species such as divers and grebes have a low learning ability, whereas sparrows and members of the crow family are said to have a high learning ability.

Lek display Gatherings of some species during breeding time, at which the males display to one another and drive off other males.

Lift The upward movement a bird attains by flapping its wings.

Mandible Jaw and bill. Sometimes applied to the lower jaw only.

Migrant Species that moves from one area to another at different times of year.

Monocular vision Seeing separately with each eye, as do birds which have eyes on the sides of their heads.

Mortality rate Number of deaths which occur in a species.

Mucus Slimy liquid substance produced in the body. In a bird this substance acts as a lubricant and helps the bird to bring up pellets.

Natal down First soft feathers of a chick on hatching or which grow soon after. It is moulted when the new juvenile plumage pushes it out.

Nestling One of the words used to describe a bird until it is full-grown and able to fly.

Nictitating membrane Clear 'third eyelid' which birds (and many other vertebrates) possess. It lies under the lids of the nasal side and can be drawn horizontally across the eye. It cleans and moistens the eyeball without shutting out the light.

Nidicolous Describes young birds which remain in the nest after hatching.

Nidifugous Describes young birds which leave the nest soon after hatching.

Nocturnal Active at night.

Nuptial display The ritual display before mating. It is sometimes called 'courtship' and varies between species.

Oil gland Organ on the rump of most birds, above the root of the tail. Also called a 'preen gland' or 'uropygial gland', and used to provide oil to smear on the plumage.

Olfactory bulb Organ that controls an animal's sense of smell. Small in most birds.

Order One of the taxonomic groups by which animals are classified. Orders are composed of families, and make up a class.

Ornithology Study of birds.

Pair-bond Bond between a male and female bird.

Passage migrants Birds which stop temporarily on their migration journey.

Passerines Birds of the order Passeriformes (perching birds); the largest of all orders of birds.

Pellet The hard lump of indigestible pieces of food, which a bird regurgitates.

Penis Reproductive organ in some male waterbirds which only appears outside the body during mating.

Population dynamics The study of bird

populations (numbers) and how they are regulated.

Powder-down Disintegrating down which produces a very fine powder helping to waterproof plumage.

Precocial Newly hatched birds which are down-covered, have their eyes open and leave the nest soon after hatching.

Predator Animal which kills other animals (its prey) for food.

Preening Method of feather care in which the bird draws the feathers, base first, through its bill. This has the effect of cleaning off dirt and lice and also fits the barbs and barbules into place.

Prey Animals which are taken for food by other animals.

Pullus (plural *pulli*) The scientific name for a bird until it is full-grown and able to fly. Other names are 'nestling' and 'chick'.

Pygostyle The fused bone at the end of the spine which is an anchor for the tail.

Raptor Bird of prey, excluding owls.

Ringing Method of marking a bird by fixing a light metal or plastic ring to its leg in order to compile records of migration, mortality rate, and so on.

Rods Parts of the eye which are sensitive to light and particularly numerous in nocturnal birds.

Roosting Sleeping, including resting behaviour when the bird is not actually asleep.

Saliva Liquid produced by the salivary glands.

Sedentary Describes a bird which does not move very far over the course of a year.

Semi-altricial Those species which are down-covered on hatching but are unable to leave the nest. Some hatch with their eyes open, e.g. the heron family and birds of prey. Others are blind on hatching, e.g. owls.

Semi-plume Small, downy feather that helps to trap warm air close to the bird's body.

Semi-precocial Those species which do not leave the nest until they are able to walk, but are feather-covered and can see when they are hatched.

Songpost Prominent perches round the perimeter of a bird's territory, from which it will sing to announce its ownership to possible intruders.

Species (plural *species*) Taxonomic group of birds (or other organisms) which does not interbreed with another group.

Sterile Unable to breed.

Sternum Breast bone.

Submissive posture Position adopted by a female bird before mating, or by a male giving way to the threats of another male.

Sub-species Population of species that is different from other populations of the same species but which will interbreed. (Carrion crows and hooded crows look different but they interbreed where populations overlap. Therefore they are the same species.)

Sub-song Autumn singing of some species, which is usually less loud and less frequent than the spring and early summer song.

Synchronous incubation Describes the incubation which begins as soon as the first egg is laid. It may therefore produce chicks which hatch as far apart as two weeks.

Taste-bud Nerve-end through which an animal tastes.

Taxonomy Arrangement and naming of groups of organisms according to their relationships with each other.

Territory Area which a particular bird occupies and defends against other birds of the same species.

Thermal Warm air column which has a tendency to rise, thus affecting a bird's flight.

Turbulence Air movement.

Urine Liquid waste matter from the body.

Vagrant Bird which occurs in a particular place accidentally, due to storms, cloud and other adverse weather conditions. Also called accidental.

Vane The area on each side of the shaft of a feather, formed by the barbs.

Winter plumage Feathers a bird grows in the autumn and keeps until its spring moult.

Zygodactylic Having two toes pointing forwards and two back.

Index
Numbers in bold refer to illustrations.